West Midlands English

Dialects of English

Series editors:
Joan Beal (University of Sheffield)
Karen P. Corrigan (Newcastle University)
April McMahon (University of Edinburgh)

Advisory board:
Laurie Bauer (Victoria University of Wellington)
Jenny Cheshire (Queen Mary, University of London)
Heinz Giegerich (University of Edinburgh)
Bernd Kortmann (University of Freiburg)
Peter L. Patrick (University of Essex)
Peter Trudgill (University of Fribourg, UEA, Agder UC, La Trobe University)
Walt Wolfram (North Carolina State University)

Webmaster: Patrick Honeybone (University of Edinburgh)

Volumes available in the series:
Robert McColl Millar, *Northern and Insular Scots*
David Deterding, *Singapore English*
Jennifer Hay, Margaret Maclagan and Elizabeth Gordon, *New Zealand English*
Pingali Sailaja, *Indian English*
Karen P. Corrigan, *Irish English, volume 1 – Northern Ireland*
Jane Setter, Cathy S. P. Wong and Brian H. S. Chan, *Hong Kong English*
Joan Beal, Lourdes Burbano Elizondo and Carmen Llamas, *Urban North-Eastern English: Tyneside to Teeside*
Urszula Clark and Esther Asprey, *West Midlands English: Birmingham and the Black Country*

Visit the Dialects of English website at www.euppublishing.com/series/DIOE

West Midlands English
Birmingham and the Black Country

Urszula Clark and Esther Asprey

EDINBURGH
University Press

© Urszula Clark and Esther Asprey, 2013

Edinburgh University Press Ltd
22 George Square, Edinburgh EH8 9LF

www.euppublishing.com

Typeset in 10.5/12 Janson by
Servis Filmsetting Ltd, Stockport, Cheshire, and
printed and bound in Great Britain by
CPI Group (UK) Ltd, Croydon CR0 4YY

A CIP record for this book is available from the British Library

ISBN 978 0 7486 4169 7 (hardback)
ISBN 978 0 7486 4168 0 (paperback)
ISBN 978 0 7486 8580 6 (webready PDF)
ISBN 978 0 7486 8582 0 (epub)

Contents

List of figures and tables

Acknowledgements

We are extremely grateful to the members of the advisory board of the Dialects of English series and to the anonymous referees for their helpful comments on the proposal for this volume. We are especially grateful to April McMahon for her suggestions for improvements of initial drafts, to Karen Corrigan for her suggestions on subsequent drafts, and to both Karen and Joan Beal for helping us through the final stages. Thanks too to Brian Dakin, who provided the transcripts for Chapter 6, and to Samia Yasmin and Anit Mahay for their research and editorial assistance. We also thank The Leverhulme Trust for the award of a Research Fellowship and the ESRC for a small grant, data from which is included in this volume. And last but not least, to Gillian Leslie for her patience.

1 Geography, Demography, Culture and Research Design

1.1 Introduction

This chapter provides an overview, discussing firstly the boundaries of the West Midlands area today within which Birmingham and the Black Country are situated, taking account of how they have changed across time. It includes a section on the demographic make-up of the region across time, before moving on to consider issues relating to language, culture and identity in section 1.5 on the theoretical underpinnings of the research upon which much of this book is based, particularly in relation to Chapters 2, 3 and 4 is also included. Section 1.6 then considers issues relating to research design, and the different methodologies adopted in research design and data collection and analysis by three separate projects which inform the chapters of this book.

1.2 The Geographical Limits of the west Midlands: Where does it begin and where does it end?

The Local Government Boundary Commission for England (2010: http://www.lgbce.org.uk/) gives the geographical range of the west Midlands as the five counties of Herefordshire, Shropshire, Staffordshire, Warwickshire and Worcestershire. The boundaries of these five shire counties date back to at least the twelfth century, being ancient subdivisions established by the Normans for administration purposes after the 1066 conquest. The shire counties were, in most cases, based on earlier Anglo-Saxon divisions. In 1974, as a result of population density concentrated in parts of the shire counties, a sixth county, that of the West Midlands, was carved out from parts of the three shire counties of Staffordshire, Warwickshire and Worcestershire.

In this volume we shall refer to the wider West Midlands (i.e. the six counties given above) as the west Midlands. The West Midlands is a more closely focused area. For the purposes of this volume, its

Figure 1.1 Boundaries of the west Midlands Area (map reproduced from the Local Government Boundary Commission for England, 2010)

boundaries are the areas of Birmingham and the Black Country, though occasionally we shall make reference to the outskirts of the area, since linguistic areas cannot be contained by economic and political boundaries. The varieties which make up West Midlands English (WME) spill over across the boundaries of the West Midlands geographical area. We turn first to defining the area of the West Midlands by defining Birmingham and the Black Country.

By the mid-twentieth century, the size of the industrial region centring on Birmingham and the Black Country and its large population led to attempts in government to subdivide the area into different boroughs, in order to give urban areas with a larger population more autonomy. The aim was to give these boroughs the power to regulate education, welfare and health services, libraries and roads. In 1966, urban, county and rural districts were created and superimposed upon, and within, the shire counties: Staffordshire alone contained over twenty urban and rural districts, plus the three county boroughs of Walsall, Wolverhampton and West Bromwich. This unwieldy system was

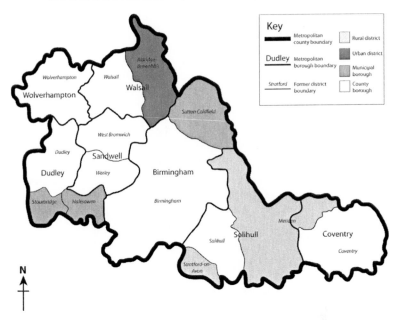

Figure 1.2 The Boundaries of the west Midlands County, 1974

replaced in 1974 with the creation of the west Midlands county. This county lingers in the national consciousness and its former spread is what many now consider as 'the west Midlands'.

This county was comprised of seven Metropolitan Boroughs: Birmingham, Coventry, Dudley, Sandwell, Solihull, Walsall and Wolverhampton. It incorporated a large part of the huge county of Staffordshire, in addition to parts of Warwickshire and Worcestershire. There are potential parallels here with other parts of the UK, where shifts in political boundaries have occurred, such as Llamas's work (2007) on Middlesbrough.

The West Midlands County Council was abolished on 31 March 1986, and its metropolitan boroughs are now effectively unitary authorities. However, the metropolitan county is enshrined in organisations such as West Midlands Police and West Midlands Fire Service, and in the divisions of voluntary organisations such as Girlguiding UK and the Scout Association. It appears on internet forms which call for an address to have a county included. For the purposes of this volume, 'the west Midlands' denotes the entire geographic area as shown in Figure 1.1, while the area to be examined in this volume is more restricted, and shown in the map of the former West Midlands county given in Figure 1.2.

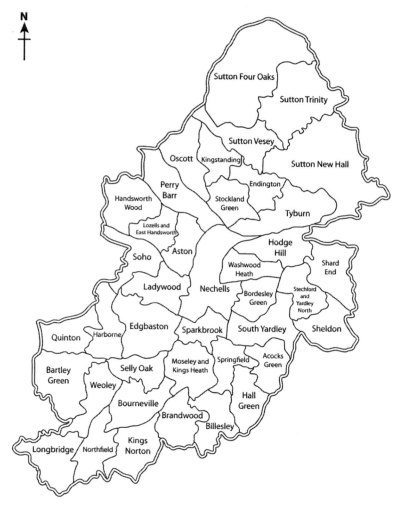

Figure 1.3 The City of Birmingham Boundaries (map reproduced courtesy of the Boundary Committee for England, 2003)

Within the geographical areas under consideration in this volume, at least two main dialect types can be identified: those of Birmingham to the east, and those of the Black Country to the west. The geographical boundaries of the city of Birmingham are clearly delineated. Figure 1.3 shows the present-day boundaries of the city of Birmingham.

Western Birmingham borders a further geographical area known as the Black Country. This area centres upon the town of Dudley and the neighbouring areas of Walsall and Wolverhampton. Defining the precise geographic boundaries of the Black Country, however, is a matter of some local dispute and debate. The most commonly cited ways of defining the area have been to use the limits of the various industries carried out in the region. Thus Gale (1966: 1) remarks that the area is 'probably as well known as it is certainly ill-defined'. He is aware that the Black Country has 'neither physical nor political boundaries' but considers that confusion need not exist, for 'if a proper basis is chosen, and if it is used logically, definition to quite close limits becomes possible'. He attempts this, yet his final decision is still distinctly nebulous. He considers that the Black Country is:

> a group of industrial towns and villages, now an almost continuous urban concentration lying to the north-west of the city of Birmingham. It is mainly in the southern part of the county of Staffordshire, though a portion lies in the north of Worcestershire, and it actually adjoins Birmingham on one side. (1966: 1–2)

Cobbett (1893: 287) referred to the area as 'the iron country' on his 1830 tour of the region, and Gale (1966: 3) agrees. The area, he says, is 'that part of South Staffordshire and North Worcestershire in which the iron trade was carried out between the years 1750 and 1900. This, it will be found, has clearly marked limits.' Sadly, Gale's map does not tally with many other accounts, including many towns and villages almost universally acknowledged as being outside the Black Country.

Over time, other historians have based their assertions on the idea that the blackness of the Black Country refers not to smoke pollution, but to coal dust. Chitham (1972: 7) gives the boundaries of the Black Country in the eighteenth century. The coalmining industry, together with the associated industries of iron making, and all the subsidiary occupations derived from the production of iron, such as chainmaking, nailmaking and lockmaking, often forms the basis of a geographical definition of the Black Country. He suggests:

> Perhaps if we take coal as a main factor in Black Country life we can arrive at a working definition of the area. The South Staffordshire coalfield stretches from Walsall and Bloxwich in the north down through Bilston, Darlaston and Wednesbury to Dudley at its centre. On the east and west lie West Bromwich and Sedgley respectively. On the south the coalfield stretches through Brierley Hill to Amblecote, then Lye and Cradley, and round in an arc from Halesowen through Old Hill to Rowley, Oldbury and Tipton. Add to these towns places where coal was marketed and used, together with parishes where the overspill population now lives, and you have some idea of the boundaries. (ibid.: 13)

Figure 1.4 The Boundaries of the Black Country (Gale 1966)

The problem is that while the very heartlands of the area may remain undisputed for linguists, residents will make fevered claims about what is the heartland of the region. A look at the BBC website and a chat forum on BBC Black Country 2008 on the subject is revealing:

Andi of the Bonk

I am from Quarry Bank. I believe The Black Country to be the areas from Dudley, Wednesbury, Tipton to Blackheath, Oldhill, Cradley, Lye and good old Quarry Bank to be the true Black Country. Wolverhampton is a seperate place entirely and Stourbridge is just outside – or so I have always been lead to believe. Seems like a lot of places are trying to cash in on what some once looked down there noses at!!!!!

DJ Andy Hicks

I agree with Andi of the Bonk. All of a sudden, all the people who used to cringe at BC, now want to be a part of it. Well its ours, an we bay gunna let it goo [we are not going to let it go]. Where is it? Dudley, Wednesbury, Oldbury, West Brom, Tipton and the like. Stourbridge, NO. Wolves, NO.

Tracey B

> I was born and raised in Old Hill and Dudley Wood and now live in Kingswinford. As far as I am concerned the road running from Old Hill Cross to the Fiveways in Cradley Heath is the centre of the Black Country if not the Universe! Forget the wannabees of Wolverhampton, Walsall and anywhere on the Birmingham side of the M5 motorway.

Chris W

> I totally disagree that West Brom or places like Blackheath were considered in the Black Country. Being born in Dudley myself, I always say that if you wasn't born within four miles of Dudley Castle, you couldn't hold the proud label of being from the Black Country. Walsall . . . Please . . .

Some contributors express strong opinions – 'e-shouting' – though their definitions also differ from ones that have gone before:

Joanna

> The 'heart' of the Black Country is . . . Blackheath/Rowley Regis/Old Hill/Cradley Heath . . . no way is Wolverhampton or Walsall in the Black Country.

Other contributors get right to the heart of the matter. Where can one say that the coal and iron (and later, steel) industries 'stopped'?

Hodgy

> Stourbridge is and was part of the Black Country. The claims that it is a separate 'market town' (and therefore not BC) are saft [stupid]. Look at any C19th map of Stourbridge and you will see iron works, pits and other related industries, just like in Dudley, Tipton etc. . . . More than anything else though, the Black Country is a cultural entity. In this sense it is pointless to try to impose a geographical limit to it.

It is clear that many people do wish to embrace the label Black Country:

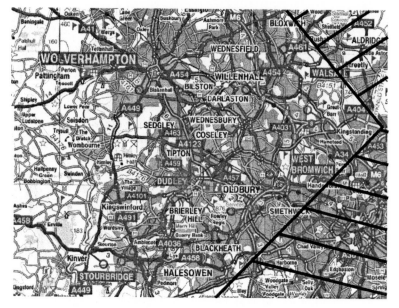

Figure 1.5 The Limits of the Black Country (dashed area excluded) (map reproduced by kind permission of the Ordnance Survey)

> Yo walsall is in da black country so i doh no wot sum of u am on a bou im black country through and through an im proud im ony 15 and i was born in da manor hospital in walsall so i shud no tnx.

(All citations from BBC Black Country 2008)

For the purposes of this volume we shall adopt a similar inclusive stance, chiefly justified by the fact that the wider Black Country and its residents share linguistic norms, as we shall see, and to exclude the boundaries of the region would be to exclude valuable structural information about the linguistic boundaries of the region. Figure 1.5, then, gives a clear picture of the area we propose to term the Black Country.

1.3 The Demographic Make-up of the West Midlands across Time

The next consideration for this section of the chapter is the effect which large-scale in-migration has had on the social structure of the area, and on the language varieties local to the West Midlands. It examines, in particular, influences in the present day from Ireland, the West Indies and the Indian subcontinent, these being some of the primary groups who have contributed to modern day population growth in the area.

The West Midlands was a key area in the inception and growth of the Industrial Revolution; in particular, the areas of the Black Country and Birmingham. Rees (1946: 133) describes the natural abundance of minerals which were to enable the Black Country to make a huge contribution to industrial development, including the fact that the most notable seam of the South Staffordshire coalfield is the 'Ten Yard' or 'Thick' coal, which reaches the unusual thickness of thirty to thirty-five feet. Underlying a large area, this seam, together with the associated bands of limestone, has been a source of enormous wealth to the district.

The Black Country also had a plentiful supply of iron ore, and is bounded by two rivers – the Tame and the Stour – which were to provide power for the mills and kilns across the region. In the later stages of the Industrial Revolution there was considerable in-migration to what is now the west Midlands from other areas of the British Isles. Between 1851–61, only a few counties showed a net increase in population by migration: the main industrial counties – Staffordshire, Warwickshire, Lancashire, Cheshire, Northumberland and Durham – as well as the London area and Hampshire. Concordantly, emigration became much more concentrated in the south-west, East Anglia and the Fenlands, and ceased to be important in Yorkshire, the Midlands, Kent, Sussex and Wales.

Economic development led to these areas becoming densely populated, and also subject to various waves of immigration from Ireland, post-Second World War immigration from Europe and subsequently the West Indies and the Indian subcontinent. The exact locations from which people came into the West Midlands may be of concern in coming chapters since it has been proposed that some brought with them linguistic features which became absorbed into the linguistic system already extant. Shropshire and Wales are cited by interested non-linguists particularly frequently as contributing to the intonational patterns of West Midlands varieties. Closer examination of the statistics for in-migration and county of origin in the nineteenth century does indeed reveal that the rural areas of Shropshire were a major source of people moving to the West Midlands region. In this way, laymen's assertions that the Shropshire dialect affected the indigenous variety may be based in fact. A glance at street names in the Midlands, for example, shows that only one instance of Salop Street as a name is found within the county of Shropshire

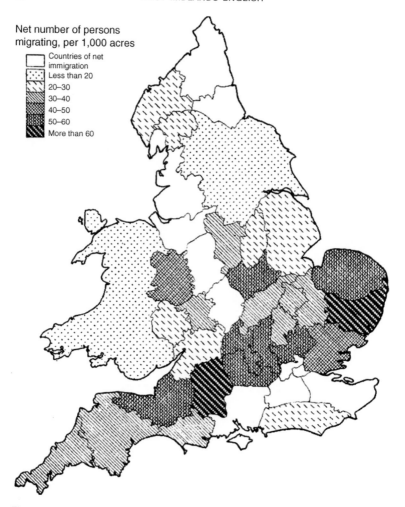

Net number of persons
migrating, per 1,000 acres

	Countries of net immigration
	Less than 20
	20–30
	30–40
	40–50
	50–60
	More than 60

Figure 1.6 Net Numbers of People Migrating 1851–61 (reproduced from
Lawton 1968)

(in Bridgnorth). The other five examples are from Birmingham,
Dudley, Oldbury, Wednesfield and Wolverhampton. Freeman (1930:
20) comments that:

> A hundred years ago two forms of dialect were in common use in the Black
> Country. Naturally they were closely akin and had many terms in common,
> but the accent with which they were spoken was noticeably different; the one
> native to the immediate district was direct and emphatic, while the other,

brought by the mining families from the neighbouring County of Shropshire was softer and intoned with a musical lilt.

In terms of immigration into Birmingham, Lawton (1968: 62) cites Cairncross (1953) in reporting that:

the volume of migration into these [urban] areas was very large, the net gain by migration alone accounting for one-sixth (17.5 per cent) of the population increase of 15.1 million in the urban areas of England and Wales between 1841 and 1911. In London, migration contributed one quarter of the total increase, and there were similar proportions in eight large northern towns (Liverpool, Manchester, Leeds, Hull, Sheffield, Nottingham, Leicester and Birmingham).

One hundred and ten years later, and despite the fact that the region's economic powers were beginning to wane, (by 1968, the last Black Country coal mine, Baggeridge Colliery near Sedgley, would have closed for ever) Champion (1976: 403) reports from analysis of census data from 1961 and 1971 that the increase in population to the West Midlands region, both Birmingham and the Black Country, at that time was still at 10 per cent and over. What is, however, instructive is what he calls the 'centrifugal effect'. In other words, the city of Birmingham itself was losing people from the city to the outer regions of the West Midlands. Between 1951 and 1961, Birmingham County Borough (as the city was then titled) lost 3,072 inhabitants who migrated (0.3 per cent), but in the following decade of 1961 to 1971 the city lost 96,013 inhabitants (8.6 per cent).

The collected population of the four boroughs of the Black Country stood, in 2001, as given in Table 1.1 below, broken down first into individual boroughs, at 1,078,318.

In mid-2008, the population of the City of Birmingham stood at approximately 1,016,800 (Birmingham City Council 2008) and that of the borough of Solihull at 205,500 (see Table 1.2).

Table 1.1 Total Population for all Black Country Metropolitan Boroughs 2001 (UK Census 2001)

Metropolitan Borough/County	Number of residents
Dudley	305,155
Sandwell	282,904
Walsall	253,499
Wolverhampton	236,582
Total	1,078,318

Table 1.2 Total Populations for all Black Country Metropolitan Boroughs 2008 (Office of National Statistics 2008)

Area	Number of residents
City of Birmingham	1,016,800
Solihull Metropolitan Borough	205,500

The conurbation of Birmingham and the western hinterland of the Black Country can be seen to have had a rich past and continue to enjoy a rich present in terms of the mix of population which choose to make these areas home. An instructive example of this diversity was published in the *Birmingham Mail* in July 2012, reporting that in one primary school in central Birmingham (Sparkhill), pupils reported thirty-one different home languages. These ranged from Urdu, Mirpuri and Punjabi through African languages including Yoruba and Lingala, to Slavic languages including Czech and Polish and on to others including Jamaican Creole and Irish. This article is a good snapshot of the linguistic diversity of all areas, and the author goes on to report that from data obtained by Birmingham City Council's education department it is clear that in the City of Birmingham over 120 languages are spoken (Keogh 2012). As a linguistic area then, the West Midlands is fascinating and diverse, and the dialects traditionally spoken here do not remain unaffected by such diversity.

1.4 An Introduction to the Language Varieties of Birmingham and the Black Country

Historically, the dialects associated with Birmingham and the Black Country link back to the Middle English West Midlands (WM) dialect, which covered a much wider geographic area (see Hughes and Trudgill 1996: 85). Black Country (BC) dialect is often considered to be particularly distinctive. Wells (1982a: 364), for example, explains that the variety is linguistically notable for its retention of traditional dialect forms such as have disappeared from the rest of the Midlands. Chinn and Thorne (2001: 25) define the Black Country dialect as 'a working class dialect spoken in the South Staffordshire area of the English Midlands', and similarly note (2001: 30) that it has 'retained many of its distinctive lexico-grammatical features'.

Todd and Ellis (1992) report that the Midland group of Middle English dialects can be considered to have had clearly defined boundaries: north of the Thames, south of a line from the rivers Humber to Lune, and with the Pennines subdividing the area into East and West

Midlands sub-areas. Brook (1972: 68) maintains that the WM dialect of Middle English (ME) was intermediate between the East Midlands and south-western dialects, with its southern part most resembling the latter. During the Old English period the region had been part of the Mercian dialect area, but following the Danish wars it came under the West-Saxon-speaking kingdom of Wessex, and retained a closer connection with Wessex than the south-west, even after the unification of England. The result is that the ME dialect resembles the East Midlands dialect in terms of early dialect characteristics, and the south-west in terms of later ones.

One project which has drawn recent attention to the WM dialect of ME is the *Vernon Manuscript* project, at the University of Birmingham (Scase 2011). The *Vernon Manuscript* is written in the dialect spoken in the English West Midlands around 1400 AD, and is said to be the biggest and most important surviving late medieval English manuscript. It was copied by two scribes, with the majority being the work of a single copyist (Scribe B), later copied and added to by Scribe A. Literary works contained within it cluster textually in ways associated with regions. Thus, the manuscript contains literary works copied in a dialect localised to Worcestershire, such as Langland's *Piers Plowman*. A further cluster relates to Staffordshire, including *The Prick of Conscience* by Rolle, the actual origin of which lies at a considerable distance from the West Midlands, and yet another localised to Warwickshire, such as Mirk's *Festial* (Horobin and Smith 2011). As part of a series of events, the project included an event called Connecting West Midlands Communities with Literary Heritage to ascertain how far people in the English West Midlands today share the language of the *Vernon Manuscript*, by reading sections of it out loud.

Recordings of the readings and a transcript can be found on the project's website: http://www.birmingham.ac.uk/accessibility/transcripts/artsand-law/english/vernon-manuscript.aspx (accessed 15 November 2012). This includes comments made by members of the public, such as the ones below:

> I have to say I'm surprised, if you'd have said to me before I read that, when I first looked at it I thought I wouldn't be able to read it at all. But as I read through there was a number of words that did actually become quite familiar and I did recognise parts of the word, all of the word, not all of them but a lot of the words. So I could understand some of it. Some of it I didn't. Some of it I could see, you know it was the way I was speaking as well, but it fitted in quite well with the words. So I didn't find it as hard as I thought I was going

to when I initially looked at it and I did cover it up so I didn't cheat at all when I was reading it so that's quite good!

Personally, I have to say that because people from the West Midlands are a bit ashamed of their accent and that you think that it's frowned upon, it's not seen as a posh accent, that if you have something like that to show you that it actually was 600 years ago that people were talking like this, that it's not something that's grown up in the last hundred years. I think it would give people a sense of being proud of our accent and the fact that we're a little bit Black Country, a little bit Midlandy, so I think it would be really interesting.

Todd and Ellis (1992) say some dialectologists consider that the ME dialect boundaries are still significant in contemporary dialect research, a point which the *Vernon Manuscript* project seems to bear out. The historians Chinn and Thorne (2001: 14–19) suggests that Birmingham was clearly within the ME West Midlands dialect area. 'Beginning as a place of some importance in 1166 when it first had a market, it was a town that was clearly embedded within its rural hinterland. For centuries it drew most of its people from the surrounding villages.' He cites evidence regarding the origins of 700 people who came to live in Birmingham between 1686 and 1726, to the effect that more than 90 per cent came from within twenty miles of Birmingham; of these, more than 200 had migrated from within Warwickshire and a similar number from Staffordshire; almost 100 came from Worcestershire and some forty from Shropshire. Of the remainder, about sixty came cumulatively from Leicester, Cheshire, Derbyshire, Lancashire and Middlesex, and another fifty from other parts of Britain. For Chinn, it is not surprising that Birmingham speech should have evolved from the dialect of north Warwickshire, south Staffordshire and north-eastern Worcestershire – essentially encompassing the ME West Mercian dialect area. In the nineteenth century, Birmingham attracted people from further afield (including Cornwall, Wales, Scotland, Ireland, Italy and the Jewish pale of settlement in Tsarist Russia), but Chinn (2001) maintains that 'local migrants continued to form the great majority of newcomers, and as late as 1951, 71 per cent of Birmingham's citizens had been born in Warwickshire'. Biddulph (1986: 1) similarly suggests that the urban conurbation of the Black Country was populated largely from the surrounding farming counties of Worcestershire, Staffordshire, Warwickshire and Shropshire.

One reason given for the distinctiveness of the BC dialect is its relative geographical isolation. The local area is essentially an 800 foot plateau without a major river or Roman road passing through it, so it was only when the Industrial Revolution got into full swing in the nineteenth century that the area ceased to be relatively isolated from other developments in the country. During the Industrial Revolution, Birmingham, Wolverhampton and Walsall grew into large manufacturing towns, separated from the centre of the plateau by belts of open land which provided raw materials for the heavy industries of the towns. Today's urban areas were originally small villages which developed with the growing industries and, with the exception of Birmingham, these still have relatively small populations. The linguistic variety of Birmingham, it might be argued, has been subject to more influences from outside the region. Examination of the ethnic structure of Birmingham at the time of the 2001 census, for example, shows that the ethnic composition of the city is not typical of that of the wider UK:

> The majority of the UK population in 2001 were White (92 per cent). The remaining 4.6 million (or 7.9 per cent) people belonged to other ethnic groups. . . . Indians were the largest of these groups, followed by Pakistanis, those of Mixed ethnic backgrounds, Black Caribbeans, Black Africans and Bangladeshis. The remaining minority ethnic groups each accounted for less than 0.5 per cent of the UK population and together accounted for a further 1.4 per cent . . . Around half of the non-White population were Asians of Indian, Pakistani, Bangladeshi or other Asian origin. A further quarter were Black, that is Black Caribbean, Black African or Other Black. Fifteen per cent of the non-White population were from the Mixed ethnic group. About a third of this group were from White and Black Caribbean backgrounds. . . . There were almost 691,000 White Irish people in Great Britain accounting for 1 per cent of the GB population. (Office for National Statistics: 2001)

Table 1.3 shows these differences clearly. Birmingham has a larger ethnic minority population than does the whole of England, when averaged out. Within these groups, it has a larger White Irish population, reflecting the arrival of many Irish immigrants in the eighteenth, nineteenth and twentieth centuries (see Chinn 2004 for more on this subject). In the same way, the Black population of Birmingham is higher than the English average, at 6.1 per cent compared to 2.3 per cent. Birmingham City Council's website holds more information on the socio-economic motivations which led to immigration to Birmingham by the Black community, particularly post-1948 when the British Nationality Act was passed, confirming right of entry to the UK for British subjects. Similarly, British subjects from the Asian subcontinent began to migrate to Britain at about the same time and for

Table 1.3 Ethnic Composition of the City of Birmingham, 2001 (figures taken from Census 2001: Birmingham)

		England (%)	Birmingham (n)	Birmingham (%)
Broad Ethnic Groupings	Asian	4.6	190,688	19.5
	Black	2.3	59,832	6.1
	Chinese, Other	0.9	11,215	1.1
	Mixed backgrounds	1.3	27,946	2.9
	White groups	90.9	687,406	70.4
Larger Ethnic Groups	Asian – Bangladeshi	0.6	20,836	2.1
	Asian – Indian	2.1	55,749	5.7
	Asian – Pakistani	1.4	104,017	10.6
	Black – Caribbean	1.1	47,831	4.9
	White – British	87.0	641,345	65.6
	White – Irish	1.3	31,467	3.2

much the same reasons – post-colonial instability meant poor wages and a lack of jobs in their own countries. The UK Census 2011 shows an increase in the 'White Groups' categories, since the opening of EU borders has led many from the former Eastern Bloc countries to seek work in England, and in many cases, to settle here. A case in point is the newly arriving Polish citizens, who are joining and augmenting the existing post-war Polish ex-pat community. The sale of Polish books in Birmingham's centrally located Waterstones bookshop, the creation of Polish delicatessens and bakeries in certain areas of Birmingham (Handsworth is a growing centre for Polish immigrants, about which more can be read at: http://www.bbc.co.uk/birmingham/content/articles/2007/01/17/polish_handsworth_feature.shtml) increasing availability of church services in Polish (the central city Catholic church St Michael's now holds Polish language mass three times each Sunday, as well as once in English) and the thriving Polish centre in Birmingham, all attest to this.

Such ethnic vitality and diversity can only add to the complexity of the linguistic situation in Birmingham. It is by no means a twentieth-century trend: from the onset of the Industrial Revolution Birmingham's population began to rise quickly and to become more mixed; and in-migration from the British Isles quickly began to change the linguistic potential of the city as new varieties were brought in.

1.5 Birmingham and the Black Country: Language, Culture and Identity

As the previous sections of this chapter have already shown, the West Midlands region within which Birmingham and the Black Country are located is geographically, economically and socially, as well as linguistically, diverse. It comprises the second largest urban area in the country through to some of the most remote rural hamlets, as well as containing some of the poorest through to most affluent areas in the UK. These places are connected to one another in many different ways. For example: through travel and journeys taken across the region to school, work or leisure activities; connections between businesses and their customers, and through common local identities. Sections 1.5.1 and 1.5.2 below provide a general theoretical context for discussing issues relating to language, culture and identity before moving on to a set of observations of what has been observed locally.

1.5.1 Theoretical Perspectives: Social Network Theory

The maintenance of local linguistic norms has often been attributed to close-knit social networks associated with working-class communities and thus, as social networks loosen or change, so too, it is argued, does the use of local linguistic norms (see, e.g., Williams and Kerswill 1999). However, increase in social mobility does not of itself necessarily lead to a disassociation with local linguistic norms. Rather, the meanings, uses and contexts associated with local linguistic norms alter, so that the norms become emblematic of identification with a particular region, rather than with a particular social class. Thus, people born and brought up in the Black Country or Birmingham (as indeed, anywhere else in the UK) who move elsewhere within England, or across the world, may still maintain links with the area and continue to identify with it. Equally, people who remain within the area but who, through factors such as increased educational opportunity and social mobility have altered their socio-economic class status, also continue to identify with it.

The expansion of education during the twentieth century in England, first of secondary schooling in the middle decades and then of higher education in the later ones, together with increased economic prosperity, has shifted the balance of the population in England in terms of social class to a point where the middle classes are now by far the largest. Consequently, as more and more working-class families move into the middle classes, it is no longer true to say that dialects in

England are linked in social terms only to the working class. Increased educational opportunity, social mobility and the media may have led to dialect levelling or a dialect losing many of its non-standard variation in parts of Britain, but this has not been the case in the Black Country, where social networks remain tight. In neighbouring Birmingham, by contrast, social networks are looser, for reasons discussed earlier. What has altered is the degree of awareness such factors confer on the Black Country and Birmingham speech communites in terms of the social values placed upon accents and dialects. This in turn leads to a more self-conscious choice of how language is used, and consciousness of how such use is affected by different social contexts. Just as visitors to Tyneside, in the North of England, will find written forms of Geordie dialect in shopping malls such as the Metro Centre (Beal 2000), visitors to the Black Country can pick up selected books of the Bible translated into the Black Country dialect at the Black Country museum, buy volumes of Black Country stories, download a Black Country dialect dictionary, and road users may be greeted with notices warning them of road works written in the local dialect.

Far from dying out then, or showing much evidence of dialect levelling, twenty-first century inhabitants of the Black Country and Birmingham consciously promote and celebrate their dialect use, especially through their speech and locally based cultural activities. Speakers of the dialect, as evidenced through the interview transcripts of Chapter 7, also show clearly that people from the Black Country and Birmingham are aware of how their dialect is perceived within Britain. Such self-awareness has been woven into the fabric of many performance texts – comedy, poetry and prose – which consciously draw attention to the dialect itself and the identity thus represented.

Sociolingusitic experiments continue to show that the Birmingham accent, particularly, is viewed negatively by others. In the latest of these (Workman and Smith 2008), members of the public were played examples of women speaking in an RP accent, a Yorkshire accent, and a Birmingham accent. Participants were also shown the same pictures in silence, with no voice to accompany them. They were then asked which of the models they found the most intelligent. In rank ordering, the women associated with a Yorkshire accent were rated highest for intelligence, above those who spoke with an RP accent. However, the women who spoke with a Birmingham accent were seen as less intelligent than any of the others – even those paired with silence. Thus, in terms of public perception, it is better to remain silent than to speak with a Birmingham accent. This begs the question as to why anyone would wish to retain linguistic features associated with the region, once they had become aware of how negatively it is perceived. The following section details a further theoretical perspective which may go some way towards answering this question.

1.5.2 Indexicality and Enregisterment

One theoretical perspective which takes account of dialect speakers' increasing awareness of regional variation in their accent and dialect is one based on the twin notions of indexicality and enregisterment. Johnstone et al. (2006: 79) argue that: 'Like languages and speech communities, linguistic locality – what it means linguistically to be "here" or "from there" and how places and ways of speaking are thought to be related – is also a product of discourse, arising as particular labels for "languages" – and their bearers.' Johnstone et al. contend that social and geographical mobility during the second half of the twentieth century have both played a crucial part in the role played by modern dialects in contemporary society (2006: 78). To this can also be added increased education and literacy rates. As increasing sections of society in modern, post-industrial technological societies are educated to higher standards of literacy than ever before, together with greater social and geographical mobility than ever before, then those sections of society whose vernacular does not correspond to that of the English used in education and other public settings, such as those related to employment – that is, Standard English – become increasingly aware of differences between the two varieties. Differences are thus identified as a particular set of linguistic features which mark out 'Black Country English' or 'Brummie', and become used consistently within self-conscious and reflexive uses, particularly those associated with writing and performance.

Key concepts in accounting for the processes associated with standardisation are those of indexicality and enregisterment (Johnstone et al. 2006; Agha 2007). The notion of indexicality draws upon Silverstein's discussion of 'orders of indexicality' (2003) which in turn echo Labov's taxonomy of the different kinds of social meanings linguistic variables can carry (Labov 1972a: 178–80). Labov traces how first order correlations between demographic identities and linguistic usages came to be recontextualised or available for second order sociolinguistic marking of social class and place. Certain of these indexical relations between linguistic forms and social meaning become, in more reflexive identity research, a resource for third order indexical use of sociolinguistic stereotypes. That is, in a pre-standardisation phase, as identified by Labov (1972a), speakers are generally unaware of variables which mark or indicate them as a member of a particular group. Once identified, such features or variables, as Silverstein (2003) contends, come to be correlated with a specific sociodemographic identity, be it region or class, for example, by cultural outsiders such as a linguist. First order indexicality, as identified by Johnstone et al. (2006), refers to the way in which the frequency of regional variants correlate with being from a particular place – Pittsburgh for example, or in this instance, the Black Country. What were indicators become, in Labovian terms, markers or norms which define a speech community and which its members use, without necessarily being aware of the variables and/or their social meanings.

Such features then, according to Silverstein, become 'enregistered': that is, they become associated with a particular style of speech. Thus, first order indexicality gives way to second order indexicality in that the frequency of particular regional variants can be correlated with being from south-western Pennsylvania, the Black Country, with being working class and, in most instances, with being male. People who are socially non-mobile in dense, multiplex social networks, do not notice these correlations, since 'everyone speaks that way'.

Markers in turn give way to a stereotype, where a specific variable feature becomes the topic of overt social comment by outsiders. It may become divorced from forms that are actually used, and thus may eventually disappear. This then gives way to third order indexiciality, where people, including those from the 'inside' such as 'Pittsburgers' or 'Black Country Folk', have become conscious of features marked out as regional, and of the fact that places and dialects are essentially linked in that every place has a dialect. Such an awareness comes about from factors such as increased education across ever wider sections of the populace and growing rates of literacy, increased social mobility, and representation of regional variation in the mass media. Regional forms are then used to mark a sense of place identity and are drawn from highly codified lists to perform local identity, often in comic, ironic or semi-serious ways. Increased education across a larger section of the population has also brought with it a conscious realisation not only of differences between dialects and the standard norm, but also of the attitudes and prejudices enregistered within various dialects of regional English in England.

Enregisterment is thus a process 'through which a linguistic repertoire becomes differentiable [and] ... socially recognised' (Agha 2003: 231). Enregisterment describes the ways in which a set of linguistic features that were firstly, once not noticed at all, secondly, came to be heard and used primarily as markers of socio-economic class, and thirdly (more recently), have come to be linked to place and 'enregistered' as a specific dialect, in this case that of the Black Country and

Birmingham. Such linguistic features can be said to have become enregistered in present-day Black Country and Birmingham dialects. Beal's work on Newcastle and Sheffield (2009) is also pertinent here, as is that of Johnstone (2009) in relation to the American dialect of Pittsburghese. Clark (2013) also discusses further indexicality and enregisterment in relation to Birmingham and the Black Country.

One example of a linguistic feature having become indexicalised and enregsistered is the forms associated with the verb 'be'. In the Black Country dialect present tense of this verb, its declension is regularised, to give 'I am', 'You am', and so on. This has led to people from the Black Country being called 'Yam Yams'. However, this term is now being appropriated by Black Country speakers themselves. In addition to these examples, it can also be said that cultural activity throughout the region is thriving, and one of its distinctive characteristics is the promotion of the arts as a regional activity. For example, there is a locally based publishing press, based in Birmingham, called Tindal Street Press. One of the driving forces behind the establishment of this press was that local writers were being told by London-based publishers that they would stand a better chance of their work being published, and thus becoming more commercially viable, if they changed the location of their work. Tindal Street Press thus established a platform for writers who were struggling to find outlets for work of literary worth which represented their own locality. Novels published by this press feature not only those written in Standard English, but also written in dialect. Although not a dialect publisher, the press encourages representations of place and location within the content of each piece of fiction they publish, with the aim of giving the reader a sense with which they may identify and with a view to raising readers' own sense of pride in the region, whether it be Birmingham, the Black Country or on a wider West Midland scale. There is also a thriving Black Country Society (www.blackcountrysociety.co.uk) which publishes a quarterly journal called *The Black Countryman*, and a local newspaper called *The Bugle*, both publishing articles, poems and stories written in the Black Country dialect. And there are regional historical societies, a Black Country Living Museum located in Dudley dedicated to the industrial heritage of the area, and featuring a wide range of local events, as well as folk bands and poets who perform their work both in Standard English and in dialect throughout the region in a wide range of pubs, clubs and theatres. The perceived distinction between 'insiders' – that is, those of the Black Country – with 'outsiders' – that is, everyone else – is manifested by the local expression: 'S/he's from off', meaning a person from outside or beyond the community who therefore may be forgiven for not understanding Black Country 'ways'.

1.6 Researching Birmingham and Black Country Dialects

This volume draws upon data collected as part of four different projects: (a) data collected in the Black Country between 2002 and 2005 as part of the Survey of Regional English (SuRE) based at The University of Leeds (see Asprey 2007); (b) data collected in the Birmingham and Black Country regions between 2001 and 2007 as part of the West Midlands Dialect Project (WMDP), in conjunction with final-year undergraduate students following programmes in English at the University of Wolverhampton and second-year undergraduates at Aston University (see Clark 2008); (c) data collected as part of two funded projects, a Leverhulme Research Fellowship project grant entitled Language and Place: Birmingham, and an Economic and Social Research Council (ESRC) small grant entitled Language, Performance, and Region: Discourse and Sociocultural Identity in the Black Country. Both these latter projects ran from 2009–10, focusing on the use of dialect in the performance of creative or stylised discourse such as poetry, comedy and drama in the Birmingham and Black Country regions. For the purposes of this book, these two projects are considered as one. Each of these data sets drew upon differing theroetical models and assumptions in terms of collecting and analysing data.

It is clear that there are variational items or forms to be found very regularly in particular dialects, and it could be that, within those dialects, some are used more by some groups of speakers than others. Consequently, this raises questions relating to issues of data collection and analysis. For example, decisions need to be made about:

- the specific social profile of informants
- whether to focus on a particular age profile of informants, or to include people from different generations
- whether to interview one gender, or include both male and female, and
- whether to mention informants from different social classes and ethnic backgrounds.

Alternatively, an approach can be taken where the specific social profile of informants is an issue secondary to the collection of data itself. For example, if the source of data collection centres on a performative event, then sampling according to non-linguistic variables associated with age, gender, ethnicity, social class etc. takes on a different dimension. The important thing to note here is that methods of data collection, and the methods used to analyse the data collected, are informed by the research questions set, rather than being bound by certain conventions without question.

So the methods of data collection chosen, and issues to do with sampling, will depend to a large degree upon the specific research questions to be investigated: for instance, undertaking a sociolinguistic interview in groups of informants or with single informants; recording speech occurring in a specific speech setting (such as a domestic one), or a more public use of speech through recording stylised performance such as plays, poems, performance poetry and comedy. There are then many different ways to design research intended to investigate variational usage. Presentation of lexical data, for example, depends on several factors, in the same way as analysis of any other part of the linguistic system would. One must consider the number of informants involved, the number of tokens collected, and any extralinguistic variables which one wishes to analyse. All three of these issues can be confronted together. Work of the kind undertaken by Pollner (1985: 11–12), which uses a system recording frequency of use in percentage terms, can only be analysed statistically if the data collected is suited to mathematical analysis. Equally, methods which give informants a word list and then a binary choice of saying either that they did, or did not, use the word, allows for unambiguous results. Data collection methods used in the projects discussed in this chapter allows some informants to give many responses, and others to give only one – or even none. Consequently, very few of the alternatives given under the umbrella of the notion word can be perceived as 'binary' in semantic terms. There is also the issue of what one calls the people from whom data is elicited. *Informant* is the preferred term to sociolinguists undertaking research in projects such as SuRE, while *participant* is the term preferred for the projects discussed in 1.6.3 which signals a collaborative venture between the researcher and those researched.

A more open approach to data collection which does not rely upon any form of word list renders itself even less susceptible to statistical analysis, and to undertake too sophisticated a statistical analysis of such data is inappropriate. As a tool for examining a newly researched community, the strength of the methodologies employed for the data discussed in this book lies in the fact that it allows qualitative discussion, thereby revealing far more about the speech community and its agreed norms of usage than would a simplified and highly structured questionnaire, or any other poll type method. More open-ended methods of data collection allow unbiased preliminary observation of patterns of usage, which then point the way towards possible explanations for these patterns.

For example, using qualitative data to investigate lexical notions individually (as discussed in Chapter 4) will be of greater value here in discovering the relationship between lexis, discourse and extralinguistic factors, than attempting to quantify lexis and analyse it mathematically. It is thus also possible to examine alternatives as being of regional significance, and to hypothesise that they might be markers of identity for Birmingham and Black Country local variety speakers and the performance artists who represent them.

The remainder of this section considers issues and methods relating to each of the projects in turn.

1.6.1 The Survey of Regional English (SuRE) and Sense Relation Networks (SRNs)

Methods used to collect and analyse lexis for this project focused upon the twin concepts of *choice* and *difference*. As Macafee (2003: 63) points out, the Labovian paradigm of research which centres upon the notion of the linguistic variable is not suited for research into lexical variation, and even less so for discourse features. This is because the ideal sociolinguistic variable 'should be high in frequency, have a certain immunity from conscious suppression, be an integral unit of larger structures and be easily quantified on a linear scale' (Labov 1966: 49). McEntegart and Le Page (1978: 110) also argue that corpus-based quantitative linguistics is concerned with variations of the same type, so that, for example, the occurrence of form A, as opposed to form B, is expressed in terms of the percentages of a common denominator from across the total stock of A and B token types that occur in any given corpus. Applying such an approach to the analysis of lexical items, for example, poses, they say, insuperable problems, since lexical types are, in their terms, 'squishy'.

Lexical items can never, it may be argued, be 'identical in truth or reference value'. To compare them on axes of stylistic variation, and of regional and social variation, it must be remembered that no two variants can be exactly alike in semantic terms, and that any comparisons must take this into account. Wolfram (1991a: 24) is content to conclude that 'choices between different content words with approximate semantic equivalence may be considered variants of a variable'. Lavandera reaches a rather different conclusion: that researchers should 'consider the possibility of dropping the requirement that "alternating forms say the same thing" and look at the social and stylistic conditioning of forms which do differ in meaning' (1978: 179).

Data collection for this project built upon these two theories, accepting that it is defensible to investigate lexical choice, and positively embracing Lavendera's conclusions that difference should form the focus of any analysis of lexical choice. Her theory supports the idea that in Birmingham and the Black Country, variation in lexical choice may correlate (in the Labovian sense) with extralinguistic variables such as gender and age.

Researchers working on the Survey of Regional English (SuRE), based at the University of Leeds, developed an approach different from that previously used in dialectology for investigating lexical usage. This new approach includes the sociolinguistic aims of monitoring language within a social as well as a spatial and temporal framework (Kerswill et al. (1999: 257)). SuRE offers linguists the opportunity to access large amounts of linguistic information about a geographical area, while at the same time offering sociolinguists the opportunity to access more detailed information about ongoing linguistic change, to allow closer study of sociolinguistic variation in a given area. The basic methodology of SuRE is detailed in Upton and Llamas (1999: 299). In summary, the more formal context of the fieldworker asking set questions to elicit grammar or lexis, such as the one employed in the *Survey of English Dialects* (*SED*), is replaced by obtaining samples of informal speech from which analyses can be made at the phonological level, and to some extent, the grammatical level as well as the lexical one.

The designers of the methodology found that an interview situation was the only practical way to elicit information on lexical data which could be compared, in ways which also reduced what Milroy (1987: 49) terms the 'asymmetrical distribution of power suggested by the roles of questioner and respondent'. Sense Relation Networks (SRNs) were thus designed to reduce the situation to something less formal than an interview situation (see also Beal 2006). SRNs invite informants to give alternative, dialect items for standard lexis, centred upon specific concepts such as 'play', 'doing' or 'being'. Informants are given an SRN sheet prior to interview, and invited to complete it, in an attempt to overcome the conflicting need to gather a wealth of comparable data at the same time as gathering informal speech, and to reduce the power imbalance of the interviewer/interviewee structure. In giving large amounts of lexical items to a fieldworker, and then going on to tell the fieldworker about those items, the theory is that the interviewee will feel that they have a more reasonable share of power in the discussion. Discussing something which informants have prepared, rather than following a structure created by a fieldworker, means that informants are interested in what they are doing (and do indeed appear to enjoy the interview). Focusing on lexis throughout an interview focuses the minds of informants on linguistic issues in general, and they are able to interact with each other with greater ease; more new lexical items occur to them over the course of an interview, than if they were presented with such questionnaires 'cold'.

In addition to the core method of the three SRNs is an Identification Questionnaire consisting of fifteen questions; its primary aim is to act as a safety net. The main aim of these questions is to elicit relatively extended responses should the informants' responses to the SRNs be insufficient for an analysis of informal speech (see also Beal 2006 and Davies and Upton 2013).

One limitation of the SuRE methodology is an extreme mental 'focusing' on lexical usage. This means that interviewers need to check exactly how many of the lexical items the informant has thought of are ones they have receptive knowledge of, and how many they actually would use themselves. There is often a disparity between these two levels, and researchers need to take care to avoid inferring that a lexical item is in widespread use just because most informants write it down.

1.6.2 The West Midlands Dialect Project (WMDP)

The WMDP was theoretically based upon a combination of (a) the SuRE methodology described above, and (b) the sociolinguistic interview. A sociolinguistic interview typically includes free conversation between the interviewer and informants, centring upon the informants' linguistic autobiography and memories, in a variety of casual and domestic settings – at home, and in leisure venues such as cafes and pubs. Informants were chosen through social networking (Milroy 1987) rather than random sampling or judgement samples. The data collection also employed a synchronic approach to data collection and analysis, in that the data was analysed for forms which were in current contemporary usage, as opposed to tracing any change across time. An important feature to be acknowledged in connection with the sociolinguistic interview is the role of the interviewer. There is still concern over the Observer's Paradox (Labov 1972b) and the extent to which the sociolinguistic interview is like 'natural speech'. One way of overcoming this paradox is to employ an ethnographic approach to data collection. Since many of the students who conducted the research were themselves from Birmingham and the Black Country, this made it possible for such an approach to be undertaken.

Consequently, the sociolinguistic interview was underpinned by an ethnographic approach: that is, an approach which studies people's behaviour in everyday contexts and uses methods to decide what possible variables might account for patterns, allowing them to emerge from the data collected (see Hammersley and Atkinson 2007), rather than focusing upon predetermined parameters such as those employed by the SuRE methodology. (See, for example, Labov 1984; Holmes and Bell 1988; Feagin 2002; Milroy and Gordon 2003; Tagliamonte 2006). The method used by the researchers pursuing this kind of data collection followed that of Johnstone et al. (2002), Johnstone and Baumgardt (2004), and Rampton et al. (2004), whereby the researcher is, or becomes, part of the community within which the research takes place. This makes it possible from the beginning of data collection to be attuned to how the areas within a specific locality, such as that of the Black Country, are understood and talked about. A vernacular understanding of local variation thus has potential implications for how particular linguistic forms are sociolinguistically deployed. Chinn and Thorne (2001: 9–10) in their dictionary *Proper Brummie* point out that:

> People like to think that there are clearly discernible cultural and linguistic differences between Birmingham and the Black Country, [but] does Brummie suddenly cease being spoken somewhere along the Bearwood Road [the main road between Quinton in Birmingham and Halesowen in the Black Country]? Does the Black Country dialect suddenly start just after the signs welcoming you to Sandwell? Of course not. The two dialects merge seamlessly into one another like colours in a rainbow, and we should be celebrating their close kinship, not squabbling about it like schoolchildren.

There is much consensus, within the Black Country community particularly, that its variety is distinct from that of Birmingham, but much disagreement as to where linguistic boundaries are to be drawn. However, the data collected as part of the WMDP and discussed in later chapters show otherwise. Although arguably not seamless, there is a considerable degree of overlap, particularly in the boundary areas. However, defining these boundaries is difficult, both geographically and linguistically, since it is well nigh impossible to ascertain where the border between Birmingham and the Black Country can be drawn.

Data collected as part of the WMDP was collected from interviews between the researchers – namely final-year undergraduate English students – and informants, in two different ways. Students were given the choice of, firstly, employing the Sense Relations Networks and SuRE methodology, described above, and secondly, the choice of employing the more naturalistic method of an informal sociolinguistic interview. It is interesting to note that students favoured the informal sociolinguistic interview approach over the SuRE methodology. The reasons they gave for this was that the informal interview seemed to give a more accurate picture of lexis in everyday use than the data collected by the SuRE methodology. Some 1,000 hours of recordings were thus obtained from over 50 informants across both genders, with an age range of ten to sixty-plus, and across the social scale. One of the negative sides of collecting data in a naturalistic way is that not every recording will give the results looked for, especially in lexical variation. However, unlike the SuRE methodology, where relations between words are chosen in advance and the interview subsequently given centres upon probable rather than actual use, lexical items appearing in this data can be regarded as in use in everyday conversation.

The advantage of training students in fieldwork methods is that it allows a greater quantity of data to be collected than by a lone researcher/fieldworker. The disadvantage though is that, despite the training, a variety of interview styles were used, with recordings of varying length. Biodata also varied in quality, although social stratification of the sample matches that of the region, in that working-class speakers dominate the corpus.

1.6.3 Language and Place: Birmingham and Language, Performance and Region – Discourse and Sociocultural Identity in the Black Country

Much recent sociolinguistic work has focused on the question of how to elicit naturalistic, vernacular spoken data, and how to evaluate the closeness of recorded data to unobserved speech. To overcome such issues, the two projects here aimed to investigate the West Midlands dialects of Birmingham and the Black Country in the context of performance (drama, comedy, and so on), and to analyse not only the language itself, but the ways in which performers and audiences construct, interpret, evaluate and relate to the performed language. Rather than thinking of dialects and accents as externally given variables of sociolinguistic variation, the approach taken views these phenomena as linked to social ideologies, and linked to strategic performativity in discourse. The notion that these are resources that language users employ differentially, therefore, is a useful way of thinking about the link between language use and achieved social group membership. Both projects were based on the same hypothesis: that stylised performance is arguably the most self-conscious use of voice, and that enregistered features of accent and dialect, such as the lexical features associated with the region, are consciously chosen and employed through performative acts such as comic and dramatic performance.

Although funded by two separate bodies, The Leverhulme Trust and ESRC, the theoretical models and assumptions of both projects are identical, as are methods of data collection and analysis. The difference between the two is that of location, with one locality being Birmingham, and the other the Black Country. Both projects follow what Eckert (2005) terms the 'third wave' of variationist theory, best exemplified in the UK by the Communities of Practice (CoP) model developed by Lave and Wenger (1991) and used by, among others, Moore (2006). This theory explores the notion that linguistic behaviour is only one part of a series of active resources which speakers can draw on to align themselves with others in their peer group and outside it, the crucial point being that individuals could be part of one or more CoP *at the same time*. Using various linguistic resources to which they have access, speakers can hold and project different identities at different times. The use of indexicality theory as a model, summarised above, bridges the gap between the supralocal and the local, taking into account speakers' differing access to differing linguistic varieties and factoring in issues of local versus national judgments about different linguistic varieties. Thus, methods of data collection here focus on what possible variables might account for patterns – phonological, morphosyntactic, lexical – allowing them to emerge from the data collected. Such an approach contributes to a shift in current thinking regarding dialect use, in that factors such as social class, gender and ethnicity are *resources* that speakers draw upon to create unique voices, rather than *determinants* of how they speak and write. This is particularly the case in acts of stylised or high performance (see Coupland 2007).

Data gathered for these projects was thus of the most reflexive kind, particularly in relation to recordings of stylised performance. Indeed, performers stated in interview that they are very well aware of the use of regional forms in their performances, including lexical items, with which their audience, being local, were most probably familiar. When performers moved out of the area, or *off*, as is said in the lexis of the area, they stated that they deliberately altered the extent of regional specificity depending upon their geographical distance from the region. Here, regionally located linguistic items, when used in performance, are used in an iconic or emblematic way, specifically in relation to the region and performances of Birmingham or Black Country regional identity.

A further theoretical approach underpinning the design of the projects is that advocated by Allan Bell in his notion of audience design (2001).

Audience design seeks to answer the question: '*Why* did *this speaker* say it *this way* on *this occasion?*' (2001: 139). The question of language style, then, makes *people* or *speakers* the focus of attention, rather than mechanisms or functions. It is therefore 'a strategy by which speakers draw on a range of linguistic resources available to them in their speech community to respond to different kinds of audiences' (2001: 145).

The data collected for both projects was obtained via attendance at a number of performance events in various venues across the Birmingham and Black Country regions, and via semi-structured interviews with performers and members of the audience. Access to performances, performers and members of the audience in Birmingham and the Black Country was made via local contacts such as comedians and theatre groups. However, in collecting data, various unforeseen problems emerged. One of these was persuading members of the audience to take part in interviews. Various performance venues would not allow leaflets asking audiences to contact us since this contravened health and safety legislation. Although very willing, it also proved difficult to pin performers down to a date and time for interviews subsequent to the performance. Consequently, fieldwork for both projects was extended to include well-known 'celebrity' performers, actors, writers, academics and broadcast journalists who had been born and brought up in the area. At the time of writing, sound recordings of performances and performer and audience interviews have not been transcribed. Instead, this section considers lexical data as found in seven interviews undertaken in 2010 under the celebrity category.

In date order, the interviews were with: Carl Chinn, Professor of Social History at the University of Birmingham; Al Atkins, a founder member of the heavy metal band *Judas Priest*; Spoz, aka Giovanni Esposito, a Birmingham Poet Laureate; Geoff Stevens and Brian Hawthorne, two of the most locally well-known writers and performers; Julie Walters, a nationally and internationally renowned actress; and Mick Pearson, editor of *The Black Countryman*, a journal dedicated to all matters of Black Country social history and culture. The participants, through education and/or geographical mobility, are clearly very well aware of differences between the accents and dialects of their birthplaces and Standard English. Nevertheless, all of those interviewed reported that they have, to varying degrees, resisted modifying their speech to conform more to Standard English and RP, and in some cases, most notably that of Professor Carl Chinn, emphasise the locality of their speech in arguably exaggerated ways. Thus, although the performers listed above describe themselves as from working-class backgrounds, five out of seven went on to higher education after leaving school at eighteen, with two educated until the age of sixteen. All of these performers point to a trend where increased education and/or increased social mobility does not necessarily lead to increased linguistic standardisation. Instead, it points to standardisation trends of a different kind, based upon regionally variant lexis once used unconsciously by its speakers, which has become emblematised or enregistered as indicative of a specific place.

Using an ethnographic approach to data collection has been found to be very time-consuming. Unlike the methods used for the SuRE project, for example, recording performances is preceded by several visits to performances to get to know the performer(s) and the venues at which they perform. Although getting permission to record performance events taking place in pubs and open air spaces such as festivals was not a problem, it was extremely difficult to get permission from other venues, such as theatres. Paradoxically, getting members of the audience to agree to be interviewed after attending an event in a pub or club proved problematic, while those attending a theatre event were more forthcoming. This was probably due to the fact that people in a pub or club were not necessarily there to see a performance, but for other reasons such as to meet friends, whereas those attending a theatre event were there specifically to see a particular event.

1.7 Conclusion

This chapter has provided an overview of the geographic, demographic, economic and cultural make-up of the Birmingham and Black Country regions. It has also provided a theoretical background for the purposes of data analysis, and a discussion of the different research designs that informed different approaches to data collection. The following three chapters provided detailed, linguistic description of the phonology, grammar and lexis of the regions, before moving on to discuss language change. The final chapters provide transcripts with linguistic and theoretical commentary, and an annotated references section.

2 Phonetics and Phonology

2.1 Overview

This chapter provides a description of the phonology of the west Midlands. The data upon which this chapter draws is taken largely from Asprey (2007) and Clark (2008) discussed in section 1.5, supplemented by the data gathered as part of the projects outlined in section 1.6. The vocalic inventory is presented in a structure based on Wells's lexical sets (1982a). An examination of consonantal variables over time follows. The chapter presents supporting evidence for patterns of use and change in progress.

Wells (1982b: 363) uses lexical sets to show the vocalic inventory of what he calls West Midlands speech. He gives (Figure 2.1) a system applying not only to Birmingham, but 'generally to the west Midlands, including the Black Country around Wolverhampton'. His sources are Painter (1963) and Heath (1971), and his table marks the most fre-

KIT	ɪ	FLEECE	iː	NEAR	iːə >ɪə
DRESS	ɛ	FACE	ʌɪ	SQUARE	ɛː
TRAP	a	PALM	ɑː	START	ɑː
LOT	ɒ	THOUGHT	ɔː	NORTH	ɔː
STRUT	ʊ >ʌ	GOAT	ʌʊ	FORCE	ʌʊə >ɔː
FOOT	ʊ	GOOSE	uː	CURE	uːə >ʊəː
BATH	ɑ	PRICE	ɒɪ	happY	i
CLOTH	ɒ	CHOICE	ɒɪ >oɪ	lettER	ə
NURSE	ɜ	MOUTH	æʊ	commA	ə

Figure 2.1 The Lexical Sets of West Midlands Speech (Wells 1982b: 364)

KIT	i	FLEECE	i:>ɪi>əi	NEAR	iə
DRESS	ɛ	FACE	æi>ɛi	SQUARE	ɛː
TRAP	æ>æː	PALM	ɑː	START	ɑː
LOT	ɒ>ɔ	THOUGHT	ɔː	NORTH	ɔː
STRUT	ɒ>ʊ>ə	GOAT	aʊ>ɔʊ	FORCE	ɔː
FOOT	ʊ	GOOSE	uː	CURE	juːə>jɔː
BATH	æ>a	PRICE	ai>ɑi>ɔi	happY	i
CLOTH	ɒ>ɔ	CHOICE	ɔi	lettER	ɛ>ə
NURSE	ɔ̞>ə̞	MOUTH	æu>ɛu	horsEs	i
				commA	ə

Figure 2.2 The Lexical Sets of Black Country Speech (Mathisen 1999: 108)

quently used variant first, showing other possible variants using the >
symbol. Mathisen (1999) produces a similar table of lexical sets from
her research in the Metropolitan Borough of Sandwell, focused on
Wednesbury and Tipton (shown in Figure 2.2), also marking the most
frequent variant first.

It could be argued that using a standard such as RP or General
American as a baseline variety for comparison might obscure the structure of the variety under scrutiny. Our decision to fit the West Midlands
system into the table is based not only on ease of interpretation, but
on the fact that the major differences in the distribution of phonemes
often (though not always) occur at the local end of the continuum,
whereas we wish to analyse and document a wider range of variation.
To use West Midlands (wM) phonology-based lexical sets would be
more complex for the reader to interpret than using Wells's sets. Where
historical developments have resulted in a differing distribution of phonemes which exist in both varieties, we make this difference clear and
comment on the axis of difference between the 'older local' and 'newer
local' forms. There is variation not only on a standard–local axis, but
also on a local axis across time; that is, older speakers often use different
phonemes in certain lexical sets to younger speakers at the local end of
the continuum.

West Midlands English is typical of a variety situated on the so-
called 'North–South' linguistic divide in England. In both morphological and phonological terms it forms a transition zone which might more

reasonably termed a Midlands dialect area. Comparison of Wells's table with eye-dialect evidence from Tennant in Birmingham (1982, 1983) proves informative. Figure 2.3 shows examples of lexical items respelled, which reinforce Wells's table. We turn now to a detailed presentation of the vowel and consonant system of Birmingham English (BhamEng), beginning with short vowels. Comment is made only on those vowels which differ greatly from the realisations they have in RP.

2.2 Short Vowels

KIT
Wells (1982a: 128) gives the RP realisation [ɪ]. He describes it as 'relatively short, lax, fairly front, and fairly close unrounded'. Painter finds subtle stratification within the set (1963: 30). He reports [i] in stressed positions, versus [ɪ] in unstressed positions. Manley too reports [ɪ] in unstressed positions versus a more open, more centralised variant [ï] (1971: 14). By 1999, Mathisen finds that [i] is the usual realisation throughout the set, but her transcription is noticeably broader than that of Painter. Clark (2008: 142) reports variation between [ɪ ~ i]. It is clear that there is variation within this set, and the indications are that this may centre on stress conditions. Thorne (2003: 90) notes that:

> Birmingham articulation of /ɪ/ . . . is perhaps the most salient and instantly recognisable feature of this accent, having a less centralised and much closer quality (= [ɪ]) than any other British English variant. The Birmingham accent also differs from other varieties in that the audible level of closeness and frontedness of /ɪ/ remains constant, whether in word-initial or word-medial position, and seldom seems to be affected by word stress or intonational falls or rises.

He also reports, in wider terms, that 'a tendency in Birmingham speech to produce [ɪ] where a schwa occurs in RP is often mocked by outsiders'. This will be seen again when we examine the happY set.

DRESS
Painter (1963: 30) reports the use of [e] in his Rowley Regis sample. Manley (1971: 16) reports centralisation and raising from Cardinal Three [ɛ] which tallies with this. Mathisen's broader transcription gives [ɛ] (1999: 108), as does Clark's (2004: 143). This variant is the only one present in Asprey's 2007 study. Thorne (2003: 89) also gives only [ɛ] for Birmingham.

KIT	ɪ	FLEECE 'Noo Strate StayShun' New Street Station [ɛi]	iː	NEAR 'yairs' Years Suggests near merger with SQUARE set at ɛː	iːə >ɪə
DRESS	ɛ	FACE Rile wie 'Railway' [aɪ]	ʌɪ	SQUARE	ɛː
TRAP 'Very Cuss Vines' Varicose veins [æ ~ ɛ]	[a]	PALM	ɑː	START	ɑː
LOT	ɒ	THOUGHT	ɔː	NORTH	ɔː
STRUT	ʊ >ʌ	GOAT 'spouse sow' I suppose so [aʊ]	ʌʊ	FORCE	ʌʊə >ɔː
FOOT	ʊ	GOOSE 'yow' you [əʊ ~ aʊ]	uː	CURE	uːə >ʊəː
BATH	ɑ	PRICE 'poil' pile [ɔɪ]	ʌɪ	happY	i
CLOTH	ɒ	CHOICE 'ile' oil [aɪ]	ʌɪ >ɔɪ	lettER 'feeva' fever [a]	ə
NURSE 'tairminus' terminus suggests [ɛː] realisation	ɜː	MOUTH	æʊ	commA 'dinna' dinner suggests [a] realisation	ə

Figure 2.3 Lexical Items

The TRAP/BATH split

Wells (1982a: 232) explains the process which gave rise to this split:

> The TRAP/BATH split became implicitly established once it was clear that
> lexical diffusion meant that some lexical items previously said with [a >æ]
> now had a long vowel ([æː>aː], later to become [ɑː]), while others, although
> involving an identical phonological environment, retained the short vowel.
> Thus nowadays in RP, in the environment _s#, we have /ɑː/ in pass, glass,
> grass, class, brass, but /æ/ in gas, lass, morass, amass, mass ... Gen Am
> [General American], however, with no corresponding TRAP/BATH split,
> keeps the same vowel in all such words.

He continues (1982b: 353):

> In the north of England the words belonging to the standard lexical set
> BATH ... are very generally pronounced with the same short open vowel as
> TRAP, namely /a/ ... Unlike the accents of the south of England, the local
> accents of the north are thus flat-BATH accents.

The perceived prestige of [ɑː] in the Black Country is noteworthy: at
the pilot stage of interviewing, for example, a female informant aged
twenty-three reported that she answered the phone at her workplace
with the greeting [gʊdɑːftənuːn], and that some of her colleagues found
this amusing, since she did not use this variant in any other BATH set
lexical items (Asprey 2001). Informants are aware of the status of [ɑː],
and some laugh openly about it: 'her sister's a little bit of a snob you
see(.)she has a [bɑːT] in the [baθɹuːm]' (Laughs).

Thorne (2003: 96) reports that there is variation between the northern [a] and the southern [ɑː] form in Birmingham, and notes a speaker
in his data who produces both variants within one sentence:

> there are certain ways in which Birmingham realisations of the BATH vowel
> differ from northern realisations. For example ... aunt, laugh and laughter,
> unlike their northern versions ... are generally realised in Brummie speech
> with a lengthened [ɑː], although this is not strictly true of the speech of all
> older Brummies. One informant produces both the northern and southern
> variants of the word-initial vowel in 'ask' within the space of a single utter-
> ance: 'It used to be you used to goo 'n' ask (=[ɑːsk]) 'im an', an' ask (=æsk])
> im erm if we can 'ave a ticket for the dinner ...'

It would seem that northern forms may be influencing the Birmingham
variety, though this is a more complex theory to prove, since the

much older traditional variant for both the TRAP and BATH sets in Birmingham was always [aː]. Conversely, Chinn and Thorne (2002: 21) comment that in other lexical sets:

> it seems ... the Birmingham accent once had much more in common with Northern British speech, but has gradually been pulled in the direction of the prestige southern variants.

Thorne (2003: 95–6) reports that Birmingham speakers find the distinction between 'long' [aː] and 'short' [a] socially salient, and that their language variety is located on the dividing line of the isogloss.

Painter (1963: 30) finds [a] throughout the two sets in the Black Country (BC). Manley (1971: 16–17) finds [a], with a back round allophone [ɒ] and a raised allophone [ɛ]. Mathisen (1999: 108) reports that in the BATH set, 'the predominant variant is a short, front and very open [æ]', and that in the TRAP set the vowel is also 'more front than the [a] generally heard in the Northern varieties'. She continues: 'the old and very long form [æːː], as in [tʃæːːmpiən] champion is heard occasionally, even among teenagers'. Wells (1982b: 364) gives [a] for both the TRAP and BATH sets, and comments (1982b: 349):

> This means that the linguistic north comprises not only that part of England which is ordinarily called the north (that is from the Scottish border south as far as a line from the Mersey to the Humber), but also most of the Midlands. It includes, for example, the Birmingham–Wolverhampton conurbation.

The distribution and salience of the older [æːː] variant recorded by Mathisen is interesting in the light of her report that its use is cross-generational. Noteworthy also is the recording by Howarth (1988: 27) in Pleck, Walsall, of the variant [ɛ] in words such as 'pan', 'man', so that, for example, 'pen' and 'pan' become homophonous – this tallies with the raised allophone reported in Manley (1971). The variant also appears in the lexical items 'ess' for 'ash', and 'ketch' for 'catch' (Fletcher 1975). Clark (2004: 143) also finds this variant in her corpus, as does Asprey (2007). In Asprey's data the variant is restricted to older speakers, and varies in height between [æ ~ ɛ]. In this way, Asprey finds [nɛp] for 'nap' (sleep) and [pæl] for 'pal'. Although Ellis (1889) finds no evidence in his two person dataset from Selly Oak in the south of the city, and Orton and Barry find no evidence of it in Hockley Heath, eye-dialect evidence from Tennant (1982, 1983) suggests that the TRAP set can appear as [æ ~ ɛ] in Birmingham as well. Thorne (2003) points out that Birmingham English TRAP 'is commonly realised at [æ̝]', suggesting the raising which Tennant's spellings suggest.

This is in contrast with areas to the west, in what is known as the Black Country, where the variant [ɒ] appears before nasals in the traditional speech variety. Fisiak (1968: 33–4) describes two reflexes from Old English (mentioned by Manley – see above) which can still be observed in the Black Country:

> 1. OE had a raised allophone [ɑ̂] in front of nasals rendered in spelling by <o> (especially in Anglian) or by <o> and <a> in the non-Anglian dialects. In Middle English this allophone joined the /o/ phoneme in the West Midland area and preserved its earlier phonemic status in the other dialects, for example con, can (OE con, can) . . .
> 2. Old English lengthened /a/ before /-nd/ developed into ME /ɔ:/ (exactly as original OE /ɑ:/, for example lo̅nd, ho̅nd in all dialects except the Northern . . . from which /a/ spread into the other dialects in the following centuries.

This reflex is most likely to appear now in place names such as Quarry [bɒnk], and in stock phrases like [giːɪtsʊmɒmə] 'give it some hammer', put your back into it, work hard. It is also heard in more common lexical items like [sɒnd] and [ɒnd]. And it is reflected in the west Midlands standard spelling and pronunciation 'mom' [mɒm] for supralocal standard 'mum' – though informants usually see this as an Americanism, it is simply the West Midlands reflex of what is traditionally 'mam' in the East and North. Sixty-five per cent of thirty-nine informants interviewed in a written questionnaire by Asprey (2007) gave the local spelling as their only response to what they called their mother.

Asprey asked about the distribution of the western Midlands form [mɒn], here dicussing with a twenty year-old female informant:

> EA: 'What about something like [mɒn] – do you hear?'
> INF: 'Oh yeah [mɒn](.)my Grandad says that all the time(.)I don't think he would ever say "man" actually.'
> EA: 'What about when it's in things like "postman"(.)"milkman"?'
> INF: 'Yeah(.)[mɪɫkmɒn].'
> (Asprey 2007: 67)

The informant's report that she associated the usage with her grandad suggests that it is older speakers who use the variant, and that it is in decline. Fifteen of Asprey's thirty-nine informants gave 'bloke' as their first alternative in a written questionnaire for the word 'man', six gave [man], while only seven gave [mɒn] as their first choice. At interview only one informant actually used the form, (whereas plenty used others like 'chap' and 'fellow' at interview, as well as 'bloke'). This is suggestive of attrition. Younger informants did give lexical items which exemplified this allophone:

> EA: 'What would you say for "dirty"?'
> INF 1: 'I can't really think of one that is particular to the area.'
> INF 2: '[ɹɒŋk]?'
> INF 1: '"Ronk", yeah.'
> INF 2: 'It can mean "good" as well though(.)I [sin] a band last night(.)oh(.) ronk band.'
> EA: [to INF 1] 'What did you put?'
> INF 1: 'I put [ɹaŋk] er [ɹɒŋk].'
> (Asprey 2007: 68)

INF 1's change from the open to the rounded variant suggests that the rounded variant may be an overt marker of local speech.

The only informant who used the variant unprompted at interview was describing the closure of a local factory. She was over 70 at the time of recording:

> These big vans was [əkʊmɪn] and [ətɛkɪn] the stuff in and they was [əliːvɪn] the [machine] guards off the front and one or two of the chaps says don't forget the guards he says [woʊɜːt] about them he says if they lose the [ɒnd] there's plenty more to [tɛkəm] over (Asprey 2007: 70)

Another item concerned with this rounded pre-nasal reflex is the verb 'laugh', which is very often realised at the most Black Country end of the linguistic continuum as [lɒf]. It is hard to know where this development arose, since the Old English (OE) and Middle English (ME) reflexes for this reflect Mercian OE [æ]. The variant may be a useful shibboleth in terms of distinguishing older north-west Midlands speech from its neighbour varieties.

Asprey (2007) gives more than three instances each of speakers in Stourbridge lengthening [a] to [aˑ]. For example:

> 'That's just happened by [tʃaˑns]'
> 'there's this weird one which(.)it just made me [laˑf]'
> 'If I was trying to make someone [laˑf]'

Both are from Stourbridge on the extreme southern edge of the Black Country. There is not enough evidence to say that such lengthening is not context conditioned, but it is interesting in view of the fact that the northern isogloss of this longer vowel would lie around this area (Wells 1982b: 354–5).

LOT

Painter (1963: 30) remarks that 'Black Country speech uses "cardinal [ɔ]" where RP uses [ɒ]'. Manley (1971: 32) reports instead the [ɒ] variant, but includes also [ä] as a possibility within this set. This variant appears in 'shop' [ʃäp], 'drop' [dräp] and 'wasp' [wäsp]. It is reproduced in much eye-dialect literature: Fletcher writes that 'God sent a strung wind wot brort kwairls frum the say, un they drapped all rahnd the camp' (1975: 51). This fronted unrounded form is still in use in the Black Country today:

> EA: 'And what did you say for "play truant"?'
> INF: 'Everybody used to be frightened to death of [stap] [stapɪn] away.'
> (Asprey 2007: 70)

The same informant talks about doing a [dɛskdʒab], showing that the unrounded variant can occur before both voiced and voiceless bilabial stops.

Mathisen (1999: 108) reports variation between low [ɒ] and lo-mid [ɔ]; context conditioning for this variation is not found. Clark (2004: 144) reports similarly 'typically [ɒ], with some raising'. Thorne (2003: 102) remarks that:

> for working-class and older Birmingham speakers in particular ... lung and long and sung and song often form homophonous pairs – the vowel sound in each word being realised as [ʊ], for example 'oh, I'll never forget this as long (=[lʊŋg]) as I live'.

Eye-dialect evidence from Tennant (1982: 21) backs this observation. He gives the example – 'rung': opposite of 'roit'. For example, 'ers done it rung', which he glosses as 'she has not acted correctly'.

The FOOT/STRUT split

Most accents of English have /ʊ/ and /ʌ/ as contrastive phonemes, as can be demonstrated by minimal pairs such as 'could' – 'cud', 'put' – 'putt', 'look' – 'luck', 'stood' – 'stud'. Middle English had no such distinction among its short vowels. The present situation results essentially from the fact that Middle English short /u/ has split into two phonemes – the current /ʊ/ and /ʌ/. This split, dating from the seventeenth century, has not taken place in the broad accents of the north of England, and only partly so in Ireland. In consequence, their local accents may have 'put' and 'putt', 'could' and 'cud', and so on, as homophones (Wells 1982a: 196–7).

The West Midlands contains both southern and northern English dialect features, and, reflecting this fact, Wells (1982b: 363) finds that 'the oppositions between /ʊ/ and /ʌ/ . . . appear to be variably neutralisable, perhaps as phonetically intermediate [ɤ]'. The FOOT / STRUT split, which is so clearly marked in the south of England, and which did not occur in many northern dialects, is only partial in the west Midlands. Chambers and Trudgill (1998: 110) term the appearance of the [ɤ] variant a 'fudge between the contending phone types [/ʊ/ and /ʌ/] . . . a way, as it were, of being at neither pole on the continuum or conversely of being at both poles at once'.

Manley gives the variant [ʊ] and describes possible lowering to something closer to [ʌ], or fronting to [ɤ]. All the FOOT and STRUT items in her analysis cluster around the 'fudge' variant [ɤ].

Painter, in the Black Country at Rowley Regis, records use of [ʊ̈] categorically for the FOOT set in his small dataset – for example, [ɪs ðə last ɹəwəl ɪn ðə bʊ̈k] (1967: 32); but items in the STRUT set he records as [o], though his small dataset only proves that this is so before bilabial plosives and dental fricatives. Mathisen also reports the situation as more complex than a matter of height or distance contrast. She finds the [ʊ] allophone throughout the study for the FOOT set (1999: 108), but notes for words of the STRUT set the rounded variant [ɒ] as:

> the most common variant for all generations . . . especially in monosyllabic words where most Northern varieties have [ʊ]. It occurs very frequently with the elderly, in all phonetic contexts (1999: 108).

She contends that definite distinctions exist between [ʊ] in the FOOT set and [ɒ], [ʊ], and [ə] in the STRUT set. Clark (2004: 139) gives the fudge [ɤ] for the FOOT set, and a rounded variant at [o] for the STRUT set from the West Midlands Dialect Project (WMDP) dataset.

The BOOK subset
Clark (2008: 145) reports that Hughes and Trudgill (1996: 55) note that there is 'a difference of lexical incidence in much of the North in that several words spelt <-ook> (the subset BOOK) have kept their historically long vowel, [uː]. This is evinced in the WMDP data, although it

is recessive.' Asprey (2007) also finds this among older speakers. One informant accommodates her pronunciation of an item to that used by the interviewer:

> EA: 'What do you call running water that's smaller than a river then?'
> INF 1: 'The [bɾuːk].'
> EA: 'The [bɹʊk]?'
> INF 2: 'A [bɹʊk].'
> INF 1: 'A [bɾuːk](.)a [bɹʊk](.)the [bɹuːk] or the [bɹʊk].'
> (Asprey 2007: 70)

The same phoneme is found before the voiceless velar stop in the recording in the Millennium Memory Bank (1999) of a male speaker aged seventy-nine years old, from Quarry Bank, who calls a hook a [huːk].

Chambers and Trudgill (1998: 111) discuss the 'fudged lect' which applies in the system of Birmingham English in what Wells terms the FOOT/STRUT split. The nature of such a fudged lect is that the Northern vowel [ʊ] is present in both sets of the word, but in the STRUT set a range of realisations from [ʊ ~ ɤ ~ ʌ] can appear. At no point, interestingly, do Chambers and Trudgill invoke the notion of a Midlands phonological system; the ideological inference could be said to be that of a 'mix' between North and South, rather than a separate Midlands system. The lack of any acknowledgement that a linguistic 'transition zone' might constitute a linguistic region in its own right is evident also in Wells's inclusion of Birmingham in his section on the linguistic North (1982b).

CLOTH

In the main, the west Midlands words which fall into the RP CLOTH set are the same as those which do so in RP. In the Black Country, Painter (1963: 30) reports 'cardinal [ɔ]'; Manley (1971: 32) reports only the [ɒ] variant.

Mathisen (1999: 109) comments that 'Long/lung and doll/dull are frequently homophones in word-pairs lists.' The development of this distribution is documented in Fisiak (1968: 34) who notes by the time of Middle English, 'wM [west Midlands] -ong>-ung, for example amung for among'. This phenomenon is well attested in the data gathered from our informants in which words such as 'wrong', 'strong' and 'long' are realised as [rʊŋg] [strʊŋg] [lʊŋg]. The phenomenon is not reported by Wells, but Mathisen reports its existence and remarks that 'for younger speakers, it is more frequent before /l/ and /ŋ/'. Manley (1971: 17) reports the use of [ʊ] and of [ɤ] in 'tongs', and of [ʊ] in 'rod' and 'strock'. One informant remarks 'I'm [frʊm] the Black Country, me', and another says 'It'd probably be very [rʊŋg] to.' Tennant (1982: 28) shows this clearly for the Birmingham variety as well, when he respells the place name Longbridge as 'Lung Bridge', and 'wrong' as 'rung, the opposite of right'.

The general realisation of the CLOTH set in Birmingham now resembles that of RP /ɒ/. However, Thorne (2003: 103) points out that 'We should also note that the vowel sound occurring in word-initial position in off and 'ospital, and word-medial position in cross, across and cloth ... is commonly realised as [ɔ:] in the speech of older Brummies, as well as in marked RP.'

2.3 Long Vowels

NURSE

Mathisen finds that a close but fairly central variant [ə̝:] is typical for teenage and elderly speakers, though the variation in teenage speech signals a marked preference for the RP-type realisation [ə:], especially with girls. This variant is also preferred by middle-class speakers in general; for some speakers, especially the elderly and working class, also a less close but quite front and [e]-like variant [ə̞:]. The stylistic variation for this vowel is very clear. While the RP-like variant [ə:] has a strong position in casual speech, the closer variant [ə̝:] has equal or higher scores in all reading styles, indicating that the local variant may carry more significance as a local/prestige/standard form than the RP standard (Mathisen 1999: 109).

Wells (1982b: 364) reports only the slightly lower centralised variant [ɜ:]. Clark (2008: 149) finds that, in common with the findings of Hughes and Trudgill, the West Midlands Dialect Project (WMDP) data suggest [œ:] as the most common realisation of this set. She suggests that NURSE and SQUARE may merge 'probably at [ɜ:]' (2004: 146). Asprey's data show, however, that the merger occurs at [e:~ɛ:]. Manley makes mention of the [œ:] variant, which she says appears in words like 'scurf' and 'shirt'. She describes this as 'an advanced form of the central vowel with marked rounding' (1971: 23).

Tennant's eye-dialect evidence (1982: 24) with its respelling of terminus as 'tairminus' reinforces Thorne's (2003: 108) remark that 'speakers sometimes ... favour the [eə] variant [in examples such as] "Now don't come on Thursday [=θeəzdi:] night".' Wells also remarks that 'there are apparently some speakers [in the west Midlands] who merge SQUARE and NURSE' (1982b: 364), but does not give the value at which the merger occurs. This is in evidence in the Black Country today as a near merger with SQUARE at [ɛː], and NURSE at [ë:] (Asprey 2007: 267). It is surprising that no previous research has discovered this, since it is neither rare nor age restricted. It is spelled with the digraph <ae>, or <ai> in most dialect literature. Raven (1979) writes 'waerd buk' for 'word book' — dictionary, Fletcher (1975: 4) writes 'wairld' for 'world' and 'bairds' for 'birds'. Asprey (2007: 74) gives the following example:

EA: 'What's your word for someone who is dirty?'
INF: [Laughs] '[dë:tiskɹʊʃ]'

She also cites an informant discussing trousers: 'I mean(.)jeans am jeans to me(.)[tiːʃɜːtsətiːʃɜːt], [ʃë:tsəʃë:t]/.'

It is interesting that in the newer compound lexical item 't-shirt', the informant uses the west Midlands standard realisation twice, yet in the older lexical item, he uses the local form. It suggests restriction of the form in semantic terms, and failure to use it consistently which might ultimately result in its neutralisation at the standard value.

SQUARE
Thorne (2003: 117) reports that in contrast to newer RP [ɛə], the usual Birmingham realisation of the SQUARE set is usually [ɜː]. He remarks that this merger with the NURSE set 'can be classified as yet another principally northern characteristic'. This appears to be a change moving into the wider west Midlands competing with the merger we shall now describe.

FLEECE
The quality of the vowel in this set is reported by Wells (1982b) as categorically [iː]. Mathisen (1999: 109) reports the use of diphthongal variants [ɪi] and [əi] which are 'often heard, especially among the elderly'. However, there is a phenomenon not listed which would seem to be a marker of young female speakers in particular, which is the diphthongisation of the set to [iə]. This is attested in our data, though not mentioned elsewhere.

Wells (1982b: 364) gives only the RP value [iː] for this set in Birmingham. He notes only small variation in this set between the value given and [ɪi]. Eye-dialect evidence from Tennant (1982: 28), however, shows that there is another realisation of this set in the city of Birmingham when he gives respellings such as 'Noo <u>Strate</u> StayShun' for 'New Street Station', suggesting that the local reflex of the FLEECE set is [ɛi] – in effect, a FLEECE-FACE merger. He gives plenty of evidence of this during his writings. Thorne (2003: 104–5) considers from his own data that the local realisation is most frequently [ɜɪ]. It is clear that the Birmingham variant is diphthongal and with a lowered, possibly centralised first element.

The other common reflex of a part of this lexical set in the Black Country concerns a failure to complete the Great Vowel Shift in the region. It means that words with the digraph <ea> in spelling do not have a FLEECE-type vowel but a FACE-type vowel. They have raised through the first stage of the shift for words of their set in Middle English from [ɛ:], but not the second, so that they are at [eɪ]. The pronunciation is not rare, and well used in the lexical item [teɪ] 'tea'. Asprey (2007) cites an informant as saying 'You want to shave [joʊ](.)you look like a ripped cinema [seit].' Even young speakers in the Black Country know the joke about going fishing in the canal and catching a [weɪɫ] which had to be thrown back because the spokes were all rusty. Asprey (2007: 74) gives two examples which show that items spelled with <ee> may also be realised with this older value:

INF 1: '[Tell her] about that celery.'
INF 2: 'Oh yes.'
INF 1: 'It was your mum and dad [wɒnt] it that overheard it – where was it, up
Great Bridge [Tipton]?'
INF 2: 'No. It was me when I went to, er, up Dudley on the market(.)and erm this woman said [avjoʊsɪn] that [sɛlərɛɪ]. It's like a [tɹeɪ].' [Laughs]

Also:

EA: 'What about cold?'
INF: '[fɹeɪzɪn], we say.'

PALM

The reflex of Old English [æ] in the modern Black Country variety is, in most contexts, [ɑ:]. The older variant in the area, [a:], which is also the reflex of OE [æ] and which also came through Middle English as [a:] (but remained at the value) is today associated with the South West. It is attested in the *Survey of English Dialects* (*SED*), where it appears invariably alongside [ɑ:]. In the *SED*, realisations like [fa:mja:d] are common from the Himley speakers.

Clark (2008: 149) also points out that 'father' and some other lexical items appear with [e:~æ:]. The item most frequently displaying this reflex in the sample is 'father'. Two informants give 'ferther' and 'fairtha' respectively on their written forms, and at interview, the latter read out his written rendering 'fairtha' with the [æ:] variant; he also reported that the [e:] variant was older, and might be well rendered orthographically as 'feyther'. Another informant remarks at interview that the realisation is typical of 'Tipton(.)ay it(.)like(.)proper deep Black Country(.) [fæ::ðə].' His lengthened vowel, accompanied with a smile at interview, indicates that for younger speakers at least, this pronunciation may not be one which they are using, and is one they consider significantly different from their own.

The THOUGHT, NORTH and FORCE sets

Since Black Country English is now overwhelmingly non-rhotic, the distinction between the THOUGHT set and the NORTH and FORCE sets (which contain vowels found before –/r/ in General American) is rendered obsolete. All three of these lexical sets, as in RP, are increasingly being typically realised as [ɔ:]. To take the THOUGHT set first, Mathisen, Wells and Painter all agree that this value is the most likely, though Painter's narrow transcription finds that the actual quality is more [ɒ]-like (1967: 32), and the West Midlands Dialect Project data give [ɒ:] (Clark 2004: 138). One difference is found in the lexical item water, which has the vowel [æ: ~ æ:ə] at the local end of the speech continuum.

The FORCE set 'has no traditional name ... it usually derives from Middle English long /ɔ:/, the same vowel as GOAT, via the Great Vowel Shift, in the environment of a following /r/ ... less commonly it derives from Middle English /o:/ or /u:/, also before /r/' (Wells 1982a: 161). Mathisen (1999: 108) gives only the long vowel [ɔ:] for the FORCE set, while Wells (1982b: 365) finds in addition a triphthongal realisation [ʌʊə], which he claims is more commonly used than the long vowel variant [ɔ:].

At the older end of the Black Country variety, words ending orthographically with <oor> and <ore> are realised with [u:ə]. This applies to place names such as Brockmoor, and lexemes of the type 'door', 'poor' and 'more'. It is likely that it dates back to a failure to lower in the Middle English reflex [u:] (see Fisiak 1968: 28), and that subsequent breaking has occurred as post-vocalic /r/ has been lost. Of all the lexemes in which this older variant is likely to occur among all age groups, 'poor' is by far the most likely, but Asprey (2007: 268) gives an informant over sixty, and from Darlaston, using the variant in another high-frequency item: 'And [duːə] you know shut the [duːə] open the [duːə].' In contrast, his wife, from West Bromwich, reported that she would use [doʊə] for door. Asprey found that only informants from the east of the region, bordering Birmingham, have the [oʊə] realisation.

The NORTH set covers RP reflexes of Middle English 'short /ɔ/ plus /r/ via the pre- as a result of pre-R lengthening' (Wells 1982a: 159). No examples of the realisation [nʊˑə] for 'nor' exist in Asprey (2007), but they have been heard from very elderly speakers. Like the CURE set, this set has variation in certain words between [ɔː~ uːə].

> EA: 'What would you say if someone was ill?'
> INF 1: '[pɔːliː]'
> EA: 'Is it [pɔːliː] or [puːəliː]?'
> INF 1: '[puːəliː]'
> INF 2: '[pɔːliː]'
> (Asprey 2007: 77)

GOOSE
Mathisen (1999: 109) reports that this set has a diphthongal variant [uːə], which she claims is 'mainly for older speakers'. One informant talks about 'pumps' being a kind of soft [ʃuːəz]. Asprey's observations suggest also that young female speakers use this variant, though there are no examples of this being so in the recorded data.

Thorne (2003: 106) remarks that RP [uː] 'is diphthongised in Birmingham articulation. Having as its starting point a close-mid to open-mid centralised position slightly lower than that for /iː/ . . . it is typically realised as [ɜu].' He remarks also that Mathisen (1999) finds diphthongisation at [uə], commenting that 'a remnant of this is detectable in the speech of older Brummies, but is absent in the speech of younger generations in [my] recorded data'.

START
Mathisen reports that realisation of this set is as RP [ɑː]. Painter (1963: 30) reports the short front vowel [a], while Manley (1971: 20) reports backing of the variant. Discussing for the moment non-rhotic speakers alone, our own data show a very low, very back [ɑ] variant, as well as a low back rounded variant [ɒ]. Realisations of long vowels in rhotic accents will be discussed in the section concerning rhoticity. Older speakers in the *SED* often show the long vowel realisation at [aː], which was discussed for the BATH set, though there appears no trace of it in our own data.

2.4 Diphthongs

FACE

Mathisen (1999: 109) gives [æi] as the usual realisation of the FACE diphthong in the Black Country – as does Painter (1963: 31) – and reports that for older speakers, [ɛi] is also in use. She reports the use of the monophthong [ɛ] among older speakers in the lexical item 'taking' [tɛkɪn]. Asprey (2007) also finds monophthongs in the lexical items 'make', 'take' and 'shake', but not in other items, indicating that such a realisation is probably restricted to a pre-voiceless velar environment, and may even be restricted to these lexical items. Mathisen reports (1999: 109) that certain realisations may be 'classed as triphthongs, as in age [æiədʒ] . . . In fact, [ə] also occurs with more diphthongs (PRICE, CHOICE, MOUTH, GOOSE).' Wells (1982b: 364) only gives the realisation [ʌi], showing the back vowel [i] as the second element of the diphthong, and the lax vowel [ɪ] as opposed to the tense [i] reported by Mathisen. Asprey (2007) reports [aɪ]. This variant is attested by the incidence of near homophones in words like 'spice' and 'space'. More confusingly, the tendency with older speakers, and those at the local end of the speech continuum, is to use a long monophthong in some words of this set, such as 'bacon' [bæːːkn̩] and 'face' [fæːːs]. This is not reported for Birmingham.

Tennant (1982: 28) gives plentiful examples of the difference between RP [eɪ] and the traditional BhamEng variant [aɪ]. 'Rile wie' for 'railway' gives two good examples of this. Thorne (2003: 110), though again using the Gimsonian symbol tradition of [æ] for what is universally acknowledged among linguists as being realised as [a] in all but the oldest RP, remarks that the realisation of the FACE set in Birmingham 'tend[s] to have a more comparatively more open starting point (=[æɪ]) than most other British English dialects'. This set is heavily remarked on as being typically Birmingham, even outside that city. One example is the Brummie joke:
Q: 'What's the difference between a buffalo and a bison?'
A: 'You can't wash your hands in a buffalo.'

Asprey (2007) shows evidence of a near FACE-PRICE merger among speakers on the Birmingham border at Lapal (near Halesowen). A twenty year-old male speaker gives the example 'cause like(.)I haven't moved [əwa̰i] or anything yet'. This suggests that the merger is more complete the further east in the West Midlands one goes.

PRICE and CHOICE

Both Mathisen and Wells report that the PRICE phoneme is frequently realised in the West Midlands with a diphthong which has a backed element, followed by a front element of a closer quality. However, Wells (1982b: 364) gives the realisation [ɒɪ], so often parodied in Birmingham speech, while Mathisen (1999: 108) gives a more complex range of realisations which differ in the degrees of rounding and backing of their first element – thus [ai], [ɑi], and, 'occasionally [ɔi]'. Mathisen reports that 'additional schwa is found in more items with this diphthong than with any of the other vowels ... Typical items are night [naɪət], side [saɪəd], time [taɪəm].' Asprey's Black Country research (2007: 80) gives examples such as 'sometimes I'll say it's my [l̥ʏntʃtaɪəm]'.

What Wells does not comment on in his 1982b description of the 'Wolverhampton–Birmingham' accent is the neutralisation or near neutralisation of the two sets at [aɪ]. He discusses at length (1982a: 209) the fact that the CHOICE set, which, he explains, consists of 'loan words, mainly from Old French', alternated between front and back realisations of the first element 'until the nineteenth century ... so that ... joined rhymed with find'. Fletcher's New Testament translation clearly shows this in spellings like 'piyntin' for 'pointing', and 'vice' for 'voice'. Unrounding is found in our own data, so that one informant talks about the notion phrase 'be [ənɑɪd] by something', a second mentions his friend who was '[paɪntɪn] at the bread rolls', and a third reports rhyming slang for having an argument:

> A bull and a cow but that's husband and wife if they start to bull and a [kæʊ] (.)or if somebody like threw [ɪz] [taiz] out the pram then you'd say he's had a cow turn.
> (Asprey 2007: 81)

Confusingly, the merger reported by Thorne (2003) for the city of Birmingham works the other way round, with the two diphthongs merging at [ɔɪ]; thus 'line' and 'loin' are both realised [lɔɪn]. This merger is not found in the Black Country, though as previously shown in Wells, near merger is to be found among some speakers at approximately [ɒɪ]. These competing mergers require closer investigation; as it is, it is reasonable to hypothesise that the former merger is kept distinct from the other by region (it being restricted to the east) and age (it being restricted to older speakers).

The most important variant of PRICE as related to change across time is the monophthongal realisation which is frequent among older speakers (61 +). It is not mentioned by Mathisen, nor is it mentioned in

Clark (2008), though Painter (1963: 31) makes mention of it as occurring in unstressed positions. He places its value at [ɑː]. Asprey found in her data that it could occur in stressed positions also: an informant discussed the place Brierley Hill as [bɹaːliːl] and reported that 'it was born dead, the [tʃaːld] was'. A second reported that being too hot was [staːflin], and even used the long monophthong in the stressed form of the first person subject pronoun. Another informant discussed use of bad language in his youth and reported that 'the [soʊʃəlaːts] used it more than the working men'. In total, six informants over sixty used the variant. It appears regionally restricted to the middle and south of the Black Country, and was not found any further north than Sedgley, but this may simply mean that a greater amount of data is needed.

Thorne (2003: 111) reports that:

> the Birmingham accent has variants of /aɪ/ ranging from [oɪ] in close-mid position to [ɔɪ]; the most common starting point being somewhere just below cardinal [ɔ] in open-mid position (= [ɞ]) and moving in the general direction of /ɪ/, for example 'I didn't like (= [lɞɪk]) it.'

This realisation is stereotyped even outside the Birmingham area. Thorne (2003: 112) continues:

> For speakers with the strongest Birmingham accents, furthermore, a phonemic merger between /aɪ/ and /ɔɪ/ often results in there being virtually no audible difference between the vowel sounds occurring in words such as five and noise, hence popular impersonations of Janice Nicholl's catch phrase on the 1960s show Thank Your Lucky Stars: 'Oi'll give it foive.'

Ironically, Retrosellers' online interview with Nicholls reports her as hailing from Walsall, which she describes as being 'in the Black Country'; the fact that the two regions share features is something which many in the UK still fail to recognise.

CHOICE

Wells and Mathisen differ in their descriptions of this set. Wells (1982b: 364) gives [ɒɪ > oɪ] as the range of possible realisations, while Mathisen (1999: 108) gives the mid-rounded vowel [ɔ] as the starting point of the diphthong, giving the diphthong [ɔɪ]. Again, Mathisen reports the use of additional schwa in items of this set in words such as 'boys' [bɔɪəz] and 'coins' [kɔɪənz].

The realisation of the CHOICE set in Birmingham is linked to the realisation of PRICE. Tennant (1982: 19, 1983: 19) gives examples of the realisation of this set at [aɪ], for example in 'ile' for 'oil', 'biled egg' for 'boiled egg', and 'a vice from the past' for 'a voice from the past' (1983: 45). Wells (1982b: 208) elaborates on this:

> Nowadays most accents, including the standard ones, make a consistent distinction in minimal pairs such as bile~boil, imply~employ. It was not always so, and there are still accents which do not maintain any such distinction ... so that, for instance, a Cockney pronunciation of tie may be identical with an RP rendering of toy.

Wells explains (1982b: 208):

> The two source types [of the vowels which in RP now fall into the CHOICE set] were /ɔɪ/, used in words such as boy, toy, annoy, oyster, noise, voice, choice, void, and those which contained /ui/, such as coin, oil, join, poison, ointment. Traces of the earlier situation [where both sets could be homophonous with bile] remain in the conservative language varieties.

GOAT

Mathisen (1999: 109) finds a backed and rounded first element at [ɔʊ], but remarks that this is a variant 'increasing in frequency with age, and ... mostly used by men'. She also concludes that a triphthongal realisation is mainly confined to men, though observation also suggests that in the west and north of the region at least, this variant is in use by women and very young children. Asprey (2007), for example, cites a response from a twenty-seven year-old in Darlaston to the notion word 'cold' as [fɹɪ̈ʊ̈əz].

Mathisen makes no mention of the long monophthong [uː]. She finds that a backed starting point at [aʊ] is the norm. Clark (2004: 150) reports that the most common variants now found range from [ʌʊ ~ ɛʊ ~ æʊ]. Asprey (2007) on the other hand reports both young and old speakers who have a diphthong with a front unrounded starting point for the GOAT set – for example, [naʊz] for 'nose'.

Painter (1963: 30–2) finds a rounded and backed realisation of the GOAT set so that the typical realisation is [ɔ̈ʊ]. He also notes a triphthongal realisation in this set [ɔwə], and the possible realisation [uː]. This latter realisation appears in words such as 'coat', 'toes', 'soap', 'stone' and 'bone'. It derives from a pre-GOAT merger Middle English [ɔu], rather than Middle English [ɔː], so it does not appear in items such as *bowl, *know and *old. It is not common any more, being restricted to older speakers at the local end of the speech continuum.

Two informants reported the word [stu:nd] for 'stoned' (drunk) (among older speakers this word refers to the older form of inducing an altered state through alcohol, whereas the majority of younger speakers reported that 'stoned' had only to do with marijuana). Asprey (2007: 82) gives the example of a forty year-old Black Country male who reports:

'I've put [koʊt] [ku:t](.)jacket(.)you know what I mean?'
EA: 'And would you say [ku:t]?'
'I'd say [ku:t] [ɑ:] [yes].'

Tennant (1982: 23) gives many respellings of this diphthong which suggest that the realisation in Birmingham may be close to [aʊ] – for example, 'spouse sow' for 'suppose so'. Thorne (2003: 113) reports, however, that 'it is commonly realised as [ʌʊ]; beginning in an open-mid back position and moving in the direction of /ʊ/'. Realisations with a front, open starting point such as that which Tennant's respellings suggest, are, Thorne argues, rather Black Country than Birmingham. It seems that to argue for one variant in either case is to ignore delicate variation which will only appear as more data about Birmingham is gathered. In both Birmingham and the Black Country the UK-wide impression seems, indeed, to be that of [aʊ].

CURE

Wells (1982b: 365) finds a range of variants for the lexical set CURE, the more usual [u:ə], and the less recorded variants [ʊə > ɔ:)]. Mathisen (1999: 108) finds a binary distinction between [ju:ə] and the less recorded [jɔ:]. Her documentation of the /j/ phoneme is confusing. It is unfortunate that Wells's lexical sets contain an item which has yod in RP. Yod-deletion in lexical items falling into the CURE set does not occur in the Black Country, though it does occur in other contexts (contrary to the findings of Hughes and Trudgill (1996)). In our own sample, there is a range of realisations from what Clark (2008: 152) terms the 'RP-type [ɔ:]' to [ju:ə].

Thorne (2003: 115) explains that:

This vowel sound has more variants than any other in Birmingham English. Realisations of /ʊə/ range from [ɔ:] through [ʊə] to [ʊa] to [ɜʊa] – depending, so it seems, upon the lexical choice, age, gender, and social status of the speaker. Gimson and Cruttenden (1994: 134) list poor, tour, sure, during, cruel and usual as examples of words in which a diphthong normally occurs in RP but are at pains to point out that Shaw, sure and shore, 'still pronounced by some /ʃɔ:, ʃʊə, ʃɔə/ are levelled by many others to [ʃɔ:] for all three words'.

He considers that the [ɔ:] variant is now the most widespread in RP, and that all but the oldest and most conservative of RP speakers use ([ɔə ~ ʊə]). He finds that middle-class speakers in Birmingham are likely to use either a diphthong [ʊə] or the lengthened [ɔ:]. He also considers that:

> Younger speakers under the influence of the RP may minimise phonemic differences between sure, Shaw and shore. Working-class speakers, in contrast, may produce homophones at [ɔ:], a number of other words such as sure, poor, cure and tour are commonly realised as [ʊa], or – as is the case in the strongest Birmingham accents – triphthongised to [ɜua]. Thorne (2003: 115)

MOUTH

Painter gives [ɛ̈ʊ] for the Black Country realisation of what was at that time [aʊ] in RP. Mathisen similarly gives [æu ~ ɛu]. Clark concurs with this (2008: 152). The only point of difference between all three reports is the level of tensing in the second element, since Mathisen and Clark report [æʊ ~ ɛʊ]. Clark also raises the issue of some kind of monophthongal realisation of the set which they find evidence for in eye-dialect respellings such as 'dahn' for 'down' and 'rahnd' for 'round'. It seems from our own data that a very common realisation of such a monophthong is [ɑ:]. This happens even among younger speakers, especially male speakers, so that one finds:

> INF 1: 'You'd either [pɑ:ns] on [əm](.)or leg it before they [sɪnjəfæɪs].'
> INF 2: "[mɑ:θ] it's your gob.'
> (Asprey 2007: 83)

Among younger women the tendency is towards breaking, so that we hear:

> INF: 'No honestly Uncle Steven(.)sit [daʊwən].'
> (Asprey 2007: 83)

The most common realisation for the set at the older end of the continuum in our own data is the raised first element of the diphthong, which is clearly shown below:

> INF: 'A [kæʊ] turn.'
> (Asprey 2007: 83)

Thorne (2003: 114) reports that:

> Birmingham realisations of the vowel sound occurring in words such as cow, house and plough generally tend to have a slightly less open starting point (=[ɛʊ]) than . . . RP realisations (=[aʊ]).

SQUARE

For the lexical set SQUARE, Painter (1967: 32) reports diphthongal [ɛə] as the usual variant. Mathisen (1999: 110) finds the monophthong [ɛː] 'for most speakers . . . [ɛə] occasionally for elderly speakers'. Wells (1982b: 364) reports only the monophthongal variant [ɛː]. The most usual variants in our own data for this set are the long monophthong [ɛː] and [ɛə]. It seems from our own data that on a continuum of standard to local, the monophthongal variant is a West Midlands standard, and the realisation [ɛə] is more localised within the Black Country.

Clark (2008: 153) reports that Painter's data may suggest a NEAR-SQUARE merger. Painter indeed reports what can still be seen clearly today − that in certain words of the SQUARE set (and increasingly fewer), there is a realisation [iə]. This realisation is blocked in certain contexts. Orthography marks different groups of lexemes out as being of a different historical origin. The variant appears only where present-day English has orthographic -ere. Thus words such as 'there' and 'where' appear with the [iə] variant − Fletcher (1975: 5) gives 'the'er' for 'there', and 'we'er' for 'where' − but realisations such as *[piə] 'pear' are not possible. Asprey (2007) reports that the lexical item most likely to appear with this allophone is 'there'. An informant, when asked about clothes in general, remarks 'I've wrote that [ðiə] about [kloʊz] in general', and another loses her place on the interview form, giving the following exchange:

> INF 1: 'To be annoyed by someone [jum] irked or riled.'
> INF 2: '[wiəz] that?'
> (Asprey 2007: 84)

There is also a tendency among younger women in particular to merge NEAR and SQUARE at the value [ɜː]. This can be most easily observed in the lexical item 'year'. Unfortunately, no examples of this competing merger exist as reported in the major studies.

NEAR

Painter (1967) has [ɪə] as the typical realisation for this set. Mathisen (1999) has the tense onset segment, giving [iə]. Clark (2008) finds that the two variants are in free variation. Our data show that the second element can be fronted, so that 'hear' is realised [iːa]. In this sense, the realisation of the NEAR set parallels that of the lettER set.

Wells (1982b: 364) gives a realisation at [iːə >ɪə] for this set. Eye-dialect evidence from Tennant, on the other hand, suggests that this set can be realised with something close to [ɛː]. This would suggest a near merger with the Birmingham realisation of the NURSE set. Thorne (2003: 89) reports that the set within Birmingham has the realisation [ɜia], which puts it in a similar position to the commA and lettER sets. Tennant's eye-dialect evidence reflects this: he gives 'ee-a' for 'hear'.

In the Black Country, Painter has [ɪə] as the typical realisation for this set. Mathisen has the tense onset segment, giving [iə]. Clark finds that the two variants are in free variation. Asprey's data (2007) show that the second element can be fronted, so that 'hear' is realised [iːa]. In this sense, the realisation of the NEAR set parallels that of the lettER set in both the Black Country and Birmingham. Observation by Asprey suggests that the situation in the Black Country may be mirroring developments in Birmingham. She reports that:

> There is ... a tendency among younger women in particular to merge NEAR and SQUARE at the value [ɜː]. This can be most easily observed in the lexical item 'year'.

2.5 Unstressed Vowels

happY
Wells (1982b: 364) gives [i] for this set, as does Mathisen (1999: 108). Clark (2004: 154) finds variation between [ɪi ~ iː]. Our own data also suggest tensing. Certainly tensing is a feature of Birmingham speech – Thorne (2003: 89) gives the variants [ɜɪ ~ iː]. By proxy, Birmingham and Black Country speech being so often confused by outsiders, it is also something which is parodied in Black Country speech. Within our own sample, certain informants, when asked to describe a Black Country accent, imitated what they claimed was a local pronunciation of the place name Dudley containing a diphthong, rather than a tense long monophthong - [dʊdlɜːɪ], or even:

> INF: 'When I came back from university working with a conservation group in Dudley(.)with a load of people from Dudley(.)or [dʊdlaːɪ].' [Laughs]
> (Asprey 2007: 84)

Wells (1982b: 364) reports that [i] is the most likely realisation of the RP [ɪ] in happY. Thorne (2003: 89), on the other hand, states that the range of variation can be between [ɜi ~ iː]. Contemporary UK websites and their readers looking at Birmingham dialect often pick on the tendency to produce a diphthongal, or a very close variant of this set; thus a poster responding to a survey carried out by CoolBrands in 2008 which concluded that Brummie was the 'least cool accent in Britain' remarks:

> Hasn't been lost on me that all those defending the 'Brummoi' accent are Brummoi's themselves. Unlike cockney and scouse though the Brummies don't think the world loves their accent. Surprised that Welsh wasn't higher though, or West Country and Zummerzet ... Geordie and Scots are far more pleasant on the ear than Brummie (shudder) Scouse (yuck) or Cockney (vile).

The lettER-commA merger

West Midlands English is, in the main, no longer rhotic. Most speakers have both linking and intrusive [ɹ] in connected speech, and the sets lettER and commA can be collapsed for such speakers. Rhotic speakers discussed earlier in this chapter displayed high levels of [ɹ] following a schwa, and they never showed hypercorrect rhoticity, so that, for example, [kɒməɹ]* 'comma' did not appear.

Non-rhotic speakers at the local end of the speech continuum often display [a] where RP has final schwa, particularly when the utterance is a question tag. Thorne also notes this for Birmingham, though having adhered to the older convention of marking what is often, even in new RP, [a] as [æ] (he gives this value for BATH), reports a lowered variant of [æ], which we can plausibly infer has the real value [a]. Certainly among younger informants [a] is common at the newer traditional end of the continuum; thus an informant gives [kɫɛva] for the keyword 'intelligent'. There is also some evidence for its being present in the older local variety, since one informant reported 'my lover' as a term of endearment, but then reported:

> But if I were thinking of that word 'lover', I would think of it not as [spells out] L-O-V-E-R but as L-U-V-A. (Asprey 2007: 86)

More about commA

In the same way as the reflex preceding historic /r/ in the unstressed vowel system is realised in RP as [ə], so the Birmingham reflex is also likely to be [ɛ] or [a]. Again, Tennant (1982, 1983) respells to reflect this. 'Geyussa gew' reflects the utterance 'Give us a go' [*give*Imp 1st Pers Obj Det Noun]

In this position it is clear that with an RP realisation, [a] would be realised with schwa [ə].

lettER

Thorne (2003: 97) makes it clear that preceding historic /r/, the Birmingham English realisations of what, in RP, is realised as [ə] 'invariably have a far less neutralised lip position in working-class Birmingham speech than in RP, being realised as [ɛ] or [a] in most instances'. Tennant's respellings (1982: 13–23) clearly reinforce this. He gives 'dinna' for 'dinner' and 'smarra?' for 'what's the matter?'.

horsEs

Painter does not record an example which shows the vowel in this set, restricted as it is to certain occurrences of the plural morpheme (namely the allomorph which ends with the voiced alveolar fricative [z]). Hughes and Trudgill (1996) give [ə] for this set. Black Country speakers in Asprey's 2007 study overwhelmingly produce [iz] for the plural noun morpheme. Mathisen (1999: 108) also reports [i] for this set. Thorne (2003: 89) reports the same value in neighbouring Birmingham. There is abundant evidence from eye-dialect to back this. Fletcher (1975: 4) gives 'waggins' for 'wagons' and 'paysis' for 'pieces'. An informant gives [ɒsn̩wagɪnz] as the way in which his friend pronounces the Tipton pub name the Horse and Wagons, remarking:

'Crock . . . he's proper Black Country(.)[ɛɪiː]' [*be*Neg 3rd Pers Sing Masc]

2.6 Consonant Phonology: An Overview

While it is clear that there is a need for one reference accent to help linguists unfamiliar with a variety to access information about that variety, and that a standard accent model (in England, RP) is often used to facilitate this, it should be remembered that the Midlands as a whole, and the Black Country, in common with other areas, contain varieties which have developed along a wholly different trajectory than the East Midlands varieties which gave rise to the variety now known as RP. With this in mind, it can be seen that many of the older consonantal differences reflect this separate development. This section will point out linguistic contexts in which historical developments or ongoing change have given rise to different reflexes, and thus show the points at which Black Country speakers may diverge from RP. We examine an

RP inventory of phonemes as a base for detailing the Black Country linguistic system more closely. Discussion is structured primarily around
manner of articulation.

2.7 Stops

Glottalling and Glottal Reinforcement
Orton and Barry (1971: 1,011) give data from Himley for the *Survey
of English Dialects*. Himley is the most southern location visited in
Staffordshire, approximately three and a half miles west of Dudley
and four miles south of Wolverhampton. There the phrase 'shouldn't
have' is recorded as [ʃʊdnt əv ədʊn], showing that [t] is fully exploded
in medial position (and also, interestingly, the residual use of the Old
English ġe- past participle marker which has the reflex [ə] in the older
local Black Country variety). Similarly (1971: 797) 'five minutes to
eight' is recorded as [faːɪv mɪnɪts tʊ ɛɪt], showing [t] in word-final
stressed position. The rarity of the glottal stop in local Black Country
speech is such that Painter (1963: 31) concludes from his recording
of darts players in conversation at a public house in Rowley Regis
(approximately two miles south-east of Dudley) that '[ʔ] does not
occur'. Manley (1971) records no instances of glottalling or glottal reinforcement in Cradley Heath.

The present day situation appears to be that [p, t, k] differ now
in their realisation medially and finally. Glottalisation of [t] is found
by Mathisen (1999: 110) to be very frequent in teenage speech, and
also variably so in young adults up to thirty years old), especially
among the middle classes; but it is very infrequent in the speech of
the elderly. Age is the main social factor, but female and middle-class
speakers, in that order, are at the front of this ongoing change. The
score for [ʔ] in word-final and word-medial position (all phonetic
contexts included) is 23 per cent for female speakers and 18 per cent
for males. The equivalent scores for [ʔ] before approximants only,
however, are 53 per cent and 44 per cent respectively. In word-final
position only, the scores rise to 58 per cent and 5 per cent, in pre-
approximant positions.

Mathisen finds the same pattern at lower levels in the realisation
of [p] and [k]. Since glottalling and glottalising are not features of
older local Black Country speech, stops and the change in realisation
they are undergoing are very important. Wells (1982b: 299) notes the
appearance of glottal realisations of /t/, even in high status 'near RP'
accents, in phrases such as 'get up' [gɛʔ ˈʌp]. Clark (2008: 157) concurs

with Mathisen that 'T-glottalling occurs especially among younger speakers.' Asprey (2001) also found higher levels of glottalling in all speakers the younger they were, and more so if they declared a class origin which was liminal and in the direction of the middle class, so that lower-middle-class speakers used higher levels than did their middle-class counterparts.

Glottalling and Glottal Reinforcement

Thorne (2003: 125–6) reports that there are:

> relatively few glottal stops in the speech of middle-aged and elderly Brummies; the words daughter and butter ... for example, both being invariably realised with voiceless alveolar plosives in word-medial position, for example [dɔːta], [bʊta]. The same also appears to apply when /t/ is in word-final position (for example it, feet, that), and when in word-final position preceding a word-initial consonant (for example get me). The situation among younger working-class Brummies is very different. In the recorded data, stops are realised in all three positions, for example [dɔːʔa], feet [fɜiʔ], get me [gɛʔ mɜi].

Birmingham English must be researched in more detail to see if /p/ and /k/ are also undergoing change towards glottal realisations.

[d]

Clark (2008: 156) reports 'written evidence for excrescent [d] following [n] in Birmingham apron "aprond/haprond"'. One informant discusses this (Asprey 2007: 66). Relating a tale of a work colleague who was in her words 'a snob', she told the interviewer about the woman's graduation ceremony, and laughed as she recounted that the woman had betrayed herself by realising two lexical items with a local pronunciation, saying 'Oh, she had her [sʊstɪfɪkɪt] [certificate] and her cap and [gaʊnd].' Chinn and Thorne (2002: 33) also report excrescent [d] following [n] in Birmingham. This occurs in words such as 'apron' 'aprond/haprond', 'gown' 'gownd', 'lawnd' 'lawn', and 'saucepand' 'saucepan.' It is not, however, a phenomenon restricted to the west Midlands. Suffolk English, for one, displays this as well; Briggs (1991) cites the folk tale *Tom Tit Tot* (a parallel to the German tale *Rumpelstiltskin*), as containing the lines:

> Well, so they was married. An' for 'leven months the gal had all the vittles she liked to ate, and all the gownds she liked to git, and all the cumpn'y she liked to hev.

It is also documented for Cockney English and Cornish, to name just two. A retelling of a traditional Christmas play in Helston, Cornwall, which was originally gathered in the 1890s (The Federation of Old Cornwall Societies: undated) contains the respelling 'And there was one in a maiden's bed-gownd and coat with ribbons, and a nackan (handkerchief) in his hand and a gook (sun bonnet) on his head.'

2.8 Nasals

Velar Nasal Plus

> EA: 'And when you say "hang on", would either of you say "[haŋ] on"(.)or would you say "[aŋg] on"?'
> INF 1: '[aŋg] on.'
> INF 2: '[aŋg] on.'
> [Both laugh]
> (Asprey 2007: 87–8)

One of the most commonly described features of West Midlands consonantal phonology is a phenomenon which Wells (1982b: 365) calls 'velar nasal plus':

> In words like sing, hang, wrong most accents have a velar nasal as the final segment, for example RP [sɪŋ, hæŋ, rɒŋ]. But certain accents of the north are non-NG-coalescing . . . in them words have a velar plosive phonetically present after the nasal, thus [sɪŋg, (h)aŋg, rɒŋg]. Words never end with [ŋ] in such an accent, at least, not after a stressed vowel; and the [g] is retained not only word-finally, but also before a suffix-initial vowel or liquid, thus ['sɪŋgə] singer, ['sɪŋgən > ['sɪŋgɪn > ['sɪŋgɪŋg] singing. It follows that singer, so pronounced, is a perfect rhyme for finger, and kingly of singly . . .

In UK parodies of west Midlands speech, velar nasal plus is one of the most salient and parodied features. In contrast, Asprey (2007) encountered Black Country speakers whose use of velar nasal plus was such as to prevent them hearing the difference between the velar nasal and the velar nasal plus stop; such speakers, when imitating the interviewer producing the velar nasal in isolation, produced the bare nasal /n/. In conversation they appeared unaware of the status of velar nasal plus on a UK level. Mathisen (1999: 111) finds that 'NG is subject to a great deal of regular stylistic variation' and goes on to remark that 'in verbal endings, for example singing . . . [n] is used on average in 80 per cent of the tokens by teenage and elderly speakers . . . but [n] is hardly present in more conscious speech.' Wells (1982b: 366) also reports that:

elsewhere, the position is somewhat more complicated. In the Black Country [ŋ] without following [g] is reported as occurring after an unstressed vowel: ['muːvɪŋ], one form of moving, used by many who would nevertheless say sing with final [g].

Mathisen (1999: 111) also describes devoicing of the final velar stop. Asprey's 2007 data corroborate this with examples like 'I can't think of [ɛniTɪŋk]' and '[səmTɪŋk] like that.' Thorne (2003: 121) reports that 'there is a good deal of difference [in the UK] between realisations of words where in writing an 'n' is followed by a 'g' or a 'k' . . . and the Birmingham variant is amongst its most well-known shibboleths'. Thorne explains that:

When in word-medial position -ing is realised as [ɪŋg] in Birmingham speech, as it also appears to be in Staffordshire, Derbyshire and Cheshire, whereas -ing word terminations have variants ranging from [ɪŋg] through [ɪŋ] to [ɪn] depending on the social status of the speaker. [ŋ] appears to be the variant favoured by middle-class Birmingham speakers, whereas both [ŋg] and [n], occasionally also [nk], appear to be favoured by working-class speakers.

Mathisen (1999: 111) reports from the Black Country that:

In teenage speech [ŋg] occurs on average in 50 per cent of conversational style tokens, and particularly with women it seems to be a local prestige form. It is clearly preferred in more conscious speech by both males and females . . . [ŋ] is used on average in 80% of the tokens by teenage and elderly speakers, but only 60% by the middle aged . . . But [n] is hardly present in more conscious speech . . . [ŋg] is virtually absent in conversational style speech, but marked in both WC [working-class] and MC [middle-class] reading style speech.

The confusing and conflicting reports from these two researchers do not take into account the grammatical categories and their effect on production. Asprey 2001 found that speakers favour the bare nasal [n] in present participial forms and in the so-called 'gerundive' forms. In other grammatical categories [ɪŋ] and [ɪŋg] are more likely to occur.

This variable clearly operates in a complex way, both linguistically and socially constrained, and above the level of consciousness in the minds of outsiders to the region; its usage is therefore of great interest to this project. The distribution of [n>ŋ>ŋg] is influenced by more than phonotactics alone. The variants are subject to age and class difference, and the patterning of the variable complex. Chinn and Thorne (2001: 21–2) find that velar nasal plus may even be a feature of young speech in Birmingham since 'it is not altogether true of older Brummies, who often do drop the 'g' sound'.

Asprey (2001: 20) observed a link between the syntactic function of a word and the realisation of velar nasal plus. In a study of twelve informants, 'all informants, regardless of class, use 50 per cent or more of the [n] variant when using a present participle form'. Both grammatical category and phonetic context are relevant to a discussion of the presence or absence of the final voiced velar stop.

Asprey's older informants (2007) have bare nasal /n/ very frequently, and not only in the present participle. Even younger informants, far from making mention of the parodied velar nasal plus forms, discussed the reduction of the final segment in writing of many present participles to [n]:

> I didn't put any [dʒiːz] on the end of them actually(.)I must say I crossed the [dʒiːz] off.' (Asprey 2007: 90)

It is too simplistic to agree that velar nasal plus realisations are the norm for the West Midlands in all social groups and in all instances. They may be linked to the younger generations, and also tied to a certain word class and morphological distribution.

2.9 Fricatives

TH-fronting

While the most regularly cited features of Black Country phonology have been discussed in the preceding paragraphs, Mathisen's survey in Sandwell found other, newer, consonantal differences between the Black Country accent and RP. Fronting of [θ] to [f], and of [ð] to [v], she reports (1999: 111) as being found among 'an increasing number of teenagers and . . . nearly categorical with some boys'. Analysis of thirty instances of voiceless TH-fronting and thirty of voiced TH-fronting among all speakers in our sample reinforces this finding. Forty minutes of speech were analysed, with analysis beginning ten minutes into each recording, to give informants a chance to relax. High-frequency words such as 'the' and 'that' were included, since even function words with the digraph contain the full forms of the relevant fricative. The sample was not split according to the position of the fricative within a word, nor by virtue of being monosyllabic versus polysyllabic words, since it is the presence or absence of fronted variants in any position which is of primary importance. The results of both voiced and voiceless TH-fronting analysis reinforce Mathisen's 1999 analysis of Sandwell speakers in that they show quite clearly that TH-fronting is a phenomenon associated with younger speakers. Analysis of voiced TH-fronting reveals that no speaker older than twenty-six used a fronted variant at all. Fronting levels of voiced fricatives for males in the 16−26 age group stand at 16 per cent, and for females in the same age group at 1.7 per cent.

Analysis of voiceless fronting reveals that higher levels of fronting are found among the 16−26 age group than were found for voiced TH-fronting. Male 16−26-year-old levels stand at 29 per cent, and those for females at 2.5 per cent. For males in the 27−40 age group, voiceless TH-fronting is present at levels of 1.7 per cent, and for females at zero. In the 27−40 age group only one speaker at all showed any fronting.

Thorne (2003: 124) reports that 'as is the case in many other working-class dialects, the voiceless labiodental fricative /f/ often replaces the voiceless dental fricative /θ/ when in word-initial position; thus throw is [fɪɹu], or when in word-final position following a vowel sound, for example fifth = [fɪf]'. Thorne's data show that the variant seems to be connected with speaker age − younger speakers use large amounts of the variant, whereas older speakers do not.

Similarly, Asprey (2007) finds that a variant of the voiced dental fricative [ð] is the labiodental fricative [v], and that this too is an innovation in the neighbouring Black Country. Mathisen (1999: 111) concurs: '[θ], [ð] for adult speakers; [f], [v] for an increasing number of teenagers and nearly categorical with some boys'. Such remarks are backed by Asprey's encounter with a nine year-old boy who encouraged a smaller child to thank someone for a present, saying 'What's the word? It starts with an 'f' . . . [faŋk] . . ."

[h] dropping

This is well attested over time in the West Midlands and widely reported in all research. It is found at very high levels in the *SED* (Orton and Barry 1969); thus 'hub' [ʁb], 'handle' [andɬ], 'hayrack' [ɛɹak]. Painter finds it in 1963, so that his informant remarks: 'I've just [ad] a look'; Manley finds it in 1971 (her's is categorically transcribed as [ɜː]). Higgs reports (2004: 290) that '/h/ is frequently absent'. Mathisen

(1999: 111) reports that 'h-dropping is typical for teenage and WC speech (all ages): house [aʊs], hundred [ʊndɹəd], and also occurs in reading style speech'. Asprey (2007) concurs with this, finding many informants who h-drop at near 100 per cent levels.

Thorne (2003: 118) reports that 'the aitch sound . . . is largely absent in working-class Birmingham English'. Thorne (2003: 119) points out that 'although /h/ deletion can occur in RP realisations of 'he', 'his', 'him' and so on in unstressed positions after a consonant sound . . . Birmingham speakers invariably drop the /h/ in both unstressed and stressed positions'.

[s] ~ [z]

There is a tendency to devoice the fricative in the lexical item 'because'; thus we hear: '[bikʊʒ] my "boxers" are my "boxers"(.)but I call my "trousers" "pants"' (Asprey 2007: 263). In a reverse pattern, at least one lexical item ending in /s/ in RP carries the final realisation of [z] in the west Midlands. It is extremely common for speakers to say [bɤz] for 'bus', and similarly in medial position; thus Asprey (2007) reports an informant saying that a phrase used when addressing an unshaven scruffy person is 'you want to shave [joʊ](.)[jə] look like a ripped [bʊz] seat'. Thus Tennant (1982: 11) gives the following definition in his dictionary of Brummie: 'Buzz: A public service vehicle – well-known form of transport in Brummijum. Plural is buzziz.'

A plausibly related phenomenon which Wells (1982b) terms initial fricative voicing, however, though it is reported in the *SED* for the southern regions of Worcestershire, is not found in the West Midlands sample.

Rhoticity

Hughes and Trudgill (1996: 39) consider that speakers of 'West Midlands English' do not realise post-vocalic /r/. On the southwestern edge of the Black Country in 1955, three informants from Himley near Dudley appear in the volumes of the *SED*: FS is a female aged sixty-three. TP is a male aged seventy-two – a retired forester. GB is a male sixty-seven year-old market gardener. All have variably rhotic accents. The locations in the *SED* nearest to Himley are Romsley (Worcestershire) and Kinlet (Shropshire). Kinlet speakers interviewed at that time had fully rhotic accents, and all speakers in Romsley used higher levels of post-vocalic /r/ than the three speakers in Himley. Both Romsley and Kinlet speakers have the post-alveolar voiced [ɻ] throughout, and acoustic analysis of the seven-minute recording made with GB show that the quality of his /r/ varies between [ɹ ~ɻ].

> FS, the female Himley informant, has the lowest levels of rhoticity of all the Himley informants. She has variable rhoticity following the NURSE set, the SQUARE set and the lettER set. She supplies the response: 'When your … cakes come out [of the oven] all black, then you say they are bəːɹnt. (Orton and Barry 1970: 512)

GB does not have [ɹ] following the START set. Like FS he has rhoticity following the SQUARE set, the lettER set and the NURSE set. He gives for example [pɛəɹ] 'pair' [ʌnloɣdəɹ] 'unloader' and [rɪkəɹ] 'ricker.'

TP has the highest levels of rhoticity of all three informants. He gives, for example, [θəːɹsti] (Orton and Barry 1970: 687), showing again rhoticity following the NURSE set, and he too has variable rhoticity in the SQUARE and lettER sets. He is also the only speaker with an instance of [ɻ] following the START set in [tʃəːɹtʃjaːɹd]. It is he who has the only two examples recorded by Gibson of any kind of retroflexion, since he gives both [kɔəɻ] and thunder [θʌndəɻ]. The speakers preserve /r/ longest following central and front vowels; it is very rare following the FORCE, BATH and CURE sets. In the small excerpt recorded in Rowley Regis by Painter (1963) there are no instances of rhoticity. Manley reports no examples of rhotic speech from the south-west of the West Midlands in the 1970s, and Mathisen (1999: 111) writes that 'Sandwell has a non-rhotic accent.'

Asprey (2007), however, reports on recordings she made in 2003 with two variably rhotic speakers, both from the south-west of the Black Country. Both their villages of origin were investigated by Manley in 1971, and though she did not record the ages of her informants, it is likely that most were aged about sixty at the time, while the informants Asprey discussed in 2007 were aged about fifty in 1971. One of Asprey's informants, born in1921, is a retired stamping engineer from Cradley Heath (itself in the Borough of Sandwell). Like Manley's informants, he is from a family of chainmakers and blacksmiths. The other informant, born in 1928, is a retired heating engineer from Lye (Stourbridge). The quality of /r/ used by the older informant varies between [ɻ~ɹ]; the younger [ɹ]. Thus one finds examples like these from the younger man:

> 'But Aynuk and Ayli was the real [pɛɚ wən?] they?'
> 'Of [kɔːs].'
> 'Dad was a [bʊkitbɒstəɹ] [sheet metal worker].'

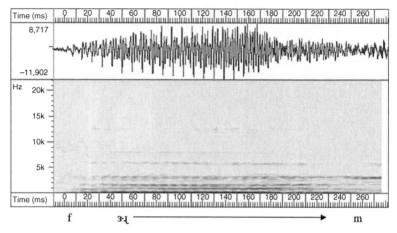

Figure 2.4 Spectrogram Showing Rhoticity in the Lexical Item 'firm'

While from the older man we hear:

'We kept [fɔːɹ] pigs.'
'She used to come round to have her [eɚ] done.'
'A tin bath in front of the [faʊ].'

The speech of a particular informant has more examples of full rhoticity, which also occurs after the FORCE and NURSE sets. This can be seen in the spectrogram reproduced in Figure 2.4, which looks at the final word 'firm' of the utterance '[bɪfɔɹ]erm, what was the name of the [fɚɹm]?' Backup evidence comes from the Millennium Memory Bank (1999). Speaker RB is from Quarry Bank, the village between Cradley Heath and the Lye. RB is male and born in 1928. He has lived all his life in Quarry Bank, and worked as a scrapyard foreman and miner.

His interview is more evidence that certain speakers still realise post-vocalic /r/. It is clear that rhoticity in the region remains longest following the NURSE set. Evidence amassed by Hubbard, working in Albrighton, Shropshire (eight miles north-west of Wolverhampton) in 1960, backs this phenomenon. Hubbard remarks that:

> When ME -er, -ir, -ur, -ē₁r -ē₂r before a consonant are represented by the central vowel [əː] almost a third of the examples occur with r-colouring, but in the other examples ME -r is lost. (1960: 204)

T-R and T-alveolar tap [ɾ]:

> The T-R rule is a widespread but stigmatised connected speech process in the middle and far north [which] involves the use of /r/ instead of /t/ in phrases such as shut up . . . [and] takes as its input /t/ in the environment of a preceding short vowel and a following boundary plus vowel. (Wells 1982b: 370)

In Asprey's 2007 data, T-R occurs, for example, in high-frequency items like the greeting form 'worro' (compare standard archaic 'what ho'), as well as the farewell 'tarra' (cf. 'ta-ta', of which the most common realisation is [trɑː]). Certainly one informant states [ʃʊɹʊp]. It is likely that the Black Country variety is on the North/South isogloss for use or non-use of the T-R rule, hence the appearance of both tap and approximant, and the coexistence of the T-R and T-[ɾ] rule. The following conversation exemplifies free variation:

> EA: 'And what do you say for "hello"?'
> INF: '[wɒɹoʊ] my dad always says [wɒɹoʊ](.)and [aduː] – that's an old one though.'
> EA: 'I think [wɒɹoʊ] is an old one as well, isn't it?'
> INF: 'Yeah [wɒɾoʊ](.)that's right.'
> (Asprey 2007: 96)

Fletcher's translation of Genesis (1975: 5) shows some kind of T to R, be it T to R or T to [ɾ]:

> Arm gunna gi' yow the privilij o' bein' gaffer oover all the livin' craychers worr arv med, but yown gorra rememba that arm the yed mon oover the lorron yer, an' if yo' dissabay me orduz ar share 'arf gi' yer sum 'ommer.

Mathisen finds that the tapped variant is 'a male variant with higher frequencies increasing with age . . . Within the female groups, this realisation is WC, and not age-sensitive.' Thorne (2003: 140) discusses linguistic change in Birmingham, and his remarks tally with the phenomenon found in the Black Country. Looking at the speech of a forty year-old man, he remarks that:

> The speaker's realisation of get his [gɛʔɪz] suggests that the influence of Estuary English is continuing to build [gɛtɪz] or perhaps [gɛɹɪz] would be expected in the speech of older Brummies.

Speakers of all ages and genders in the Black Country certainly do apply the T to R rule, but among younger ages it is now, as in Birmingham, in direct competition with glottalling. Asprey (2007: 122) found that among a twelve-speaker sample of working-class speakers in the Black Country, the pattern which emerges most clearly is the link between the age and increased use of t-glottalling. The glottal variant is undoubtedly the preserve of the youngest age group, and two out of the three informants from the other age groups who use the variant are female. Use of this variant is particularly high among the young female informants, at 53.3 per cent and 90 per cent respectively. Even among young males the percentage is higher than it is among males in the middle and old cohorts. Use of the glottal plummets to 3.3 per cent among middle males, and zero among older men.

2.10 Approximants

[l]

In all positions within the syllable, though particularly in syllable final position, male informants in particular may demonstrate the use of a heavily velarised or even pharyngealised [lˤ] (pharyngealised [lˤ] does seem to be restricted to older informants). A velarised realisation can even occur following central and front vowels, as Asprey (2007: 97) shows: 'Grassing or [tɛɫɪŋg] yeah [tɛɫɪn].' – and more in keeping with what we might expect, following schwa – 'No I didn't [aktʃəɫɪ].'

As regards pharyngealised [lˤ], Asprey (2007) gives a clear example: 'The one now from the past was "wench", but is not now(.)You very [rɛəlˤl] ever ... I very [rɛəlˤi] ever hear it now.' Even younger informants use the variant, however, so that we hear: 'Yes [aktʃəlˤiː].'

[l] vocalisation

This is widespread across genders and age groups in working-class speech. Manley remarks that 'In BBCD [Broad Black Country Dialect] the "l" is not pronounced.' The context for /l/ vocalisation she gives as coda /l/ + /d/ – it does not appear to be vocalised anywhere else in Manley's sample (not, for instance before the velar stop /k/ in a word like [mɪɫk]. She gives, therefore, only words like 'cold' [koʊd], 'told' and 'old'. These are frequently given in Asprey (2007), and the written concept words 'father' and 'partner' elicit written alternatives like 'ode mon'.

Mathisen (1999) finds, however, that l-vocalisation is a common feature, especially in younger speakers and in highly conscious speech such as the reading of word lists. It also occurs in word-final position [maɪʊ] 'mile'; word-medial position [tʃiʊdɹən]; and as a syllabic consonant [sæikʊkɹɪns] 'cycle-cross'.

Asprey cites a seventeen year-old female who gives [stɹbʊ] for 'stubble', for example, and a twenty year-old female who says 'If I'm with [sɜʔtŋpiːpʊ]'. This more widespread usage in a larger number of phonetic contexts is not one historically associated with the area. Mathisen is the first to report it. Asprey (2007) shows that velarised 'dark' [ł] can even occur word initially before a front vowel:

'I say [mi] eyes when I'm [tɛkɪn] me contact [łɛnziz] out.'
'On the [łɛft].'
(Asprey 2007: 98)

In Birmingham, Thorne (2003: 126) finds that /l/ in word-final position after a vowel (for example, 'full', 'final', 'pale') and after a vowel, but preceding a consonant (for example 'stilt', 'cold', 'help') is always dark (= [ł]), whereas in word-initial (for example, 'life', 'laugh', 'loss'), post-initial (for example, 'blast', 'class', 'sleep'), word-medial (for example, 'follow', 'silly', 'foolish') and word-final position before a following vowel (for example, 'pull out', 'full up', 'fall in') is always clear (= [l]).

Zero realisation of [j]

Hughes and Trudgill (1996: 39) claim that there is no yod-deletion in words such as few /fjuː/. Manley (1971: 40) reports that the usual realisation of this set is '[juː]; for example, "few", "dew".' Mathisen (1999: 111), however, states that in Sandwell 'J-dropping does appear (especially with new [nuː]). It is more frequent in teenage speech but also present in the speech of the elderly, and when reading.' Yod-deletion is therefore reported as a socially significant phenomenon in Sandwell, connected to both age and interview style. It is found by Asprey (2007) among all age groups, thus:

'That's me(.)that's [mi] own [stʊːpɪd] term.'
'I [pɹɪzuːm].'
(Asprey 2007: 99)

Yod-dropping is also common in BhamEng; Tennant's (1982: 28) rendering of New Street Station as 'Noo Strate StayShun' showing this clearly.

Zero initial [w]

Historically /w/ is often absent in word-initial position in Midlands and south-western varieties. Manley's verb paradigms clearly show this; she gives [wiː'ɹɫ] for 'we will' (1971: 42). Asprey 2007 reports restricted knowledge of this. Five informants (all in the age group 41–60, or older) give various respellings of [ʊmən] for 'woman'. The most northerly of these informants grew up in Darlaston, which indicates that the reflex was once present over a wider area.

2.11 Conclusion

Change over time is in evidence in the West Midlands variety. Prenasal [ɒ] in words which, in RP, contain the [a] phoneme, for example, is now more rarely found in speech, though it remains as a clear marker in eye-dialect publications. On a consonantal level, linguistic innovations suggested by others as evidence of dialect contact, in particular Kerswill and Williams (2000), such as the glottal stop, can be seen to be present in the speech of younger informants, but are only present at very low levels in the speech of the eldest informants. In the case of the phenomenon known as TH-fronting, the fronting of [T] to [f] is not in evidence at all in those over forty. A dialectological approach combining data with regional data showing the movement of people into the area might shed light on the rise of a variant which only began to be reported in the area by Mathisen (1999) in her data from the early nineties.

Age-graded change is suggested in the patterning of velar nasal plus in the Black Country. It appears that speakers over sixty use higher levels of bare nasal [n] in all contexts (present participle, noun or adjective) than do other age groups. Younger speakers, it seems, use higher levels of [ŋg] in nouns ending [ŋ] in RP, and may also use more in present participle constructions. As we have seen, however, younger speakers were often keen to express their use of the bare nasal in the present participle forms like 'chucking it down' for rain heavily, giving their orthographic rendering of the alternative as 'chuckin it down'. A closer examination of the stratification of the variants [n~ŋ~ŋg] not only by age, but by grammatical function, will shed more light on this pattern of change over time. Since it is generally considered by the wider public to be a major shibboleth of Birmingham speech, such an investigation could reasonably concern itself with contact between the Black Country and Birmingham speech communities, and with examining the Birmingham variety over time to see if velar nasal plus use has historically been found at higher levels among that speech community than it has in the Black Country. Certainly Painter (1963: 32) suggests that there is a difference between the two speech varieties linked to position of an item in a particular utterance, in that 'phrase final [ɪn] contrasts with the Birmingham [ɪŋg]'.

Loss of variants over time is also attested by Asprey (2007). Speakers' knowledge of the historically western Midlands form zero [w] shows that attrition is in some cases slow to lead to total loss of knowledge about a variant which is now very rare in speech. Similarly, Wells's comment (1982b: 364) that the Black Country is 'notable for its retention of traditional dialect forms such as have disappeared from the rest of the Midlands' remains true. For forty years, the phenomenon of rhoticity has remained uncommented on. Its continuing (albeit recessive) presence in the area is indicative of a region of the UK deserving of closer attention from dialectologists.

There is also stability across the generations for some features reported by previous research as being typical of the area. 'h' dropping is present for all generations.

The relationship between the FOOT and STRUT sets does not suggest that these two sets produce a typical northern use of [ʊ] across the two sets, though there are indeed some speakers for whom these two sets are homophonous. Instead of the usage across England suddenly and categorically becoming 'Northern', speakers in the Black Country have been shown to vary their pronunciation of the STRUT set, as Wells (1982b: 363) had remarked. There is a continuum of height difference from [ʌ] to the intermediate [ɤ], and on to [ʊ]. There is also evidence that many speakers have a rounded variant [ɒ] for many items which, in RP, fall into the STRUT set. In regional terms, the continuum is a strong marker of Midlands speech as a pan-regional variety distinct from that of the North or South.

3 Grammar

3.1 Introduction

We open this chapter concerning the grammar of Birmingham and Black Country (BC) English by reminding readers that, within any dialect speech community, speakers have access (albeit to varying degrees depending on exposure throughout their lives to different varieties) to a range of structures along what we can term a continuum, with in this case the Birmingham and BC local varieties at one end and standard West Midlands English at the other. It is important to remember in this chapter that although we will analyse grammatical structures, we are not compelled in doing so to make constant reference to Standard English (StEng), and that most speakers in the West Midlands are not standard southern English speakers.

A poll run by the BBC Voices site in 2005, reported on by the BBC Black Country Voices site Have Your Say, asked chatroom users which accent was 'the worst in Britain':

> There is nothing wrong with our accent, it's the weirdos that come from outside the Midlands that have a weird accent. Ours is a very old way of speaking this is why people take the 'p' out of the way we talk, I don't care though I'm from Wolverhampton and I'm proud of it.
> Lucy, Wolverhampton

> The Black country language is one of the oldest still surviving in England we should be proud of it! Im from the black country and from an early age my grandad used to sit me on his knee and talk to me in the black country dialect explaining what the different words meant.
> Kat, London

> I cant believe that the black country accent has been voted the worst it is proper old English.
> Michael, Stourbridge

There ai't many blokes moore black country than me. My Grandad was on the chain and anchor forging gangs that med the anchors and chairn fu the Titanic, up at Noah Hingley's. I was born and bred in Quorry Bonk, and that's the REAL centre of the Black Country. Dun the folk who criticise us not know that the Black Country dialect is the oldest in Britain, and all the other dialects stem from FOREIGNERS! The Black Country is unique, and the accent is just great.

Anonymous post

It is clear from the replies which appeared on the Black Country board that most users were also discussing the grammar and lexis of the dialect. They discussed issues such as paradigm levelling and the use of contracted auxiliaries, and looked at lexical items. The theme which was returned to again and again was that of the respect they have for the variety as an extremely old and pure form of English. We will examine these claims by tracing change in the variety, taking issue with the view that the variety is 'pure' and with the opinion of some linguists that the variety is becoming 'impure'. There has always been variation in the local Black Country and Birmingham varieties and a continuum of more and less removed from a standard West Midlands English. In this chapter, where it is appropriate (especially where verb morphology is concerned), grammatical structures will be analysed in their own right, using the conventions familiar to those working with pidgin and creole languages. These allow the formal structure to be explained exactly; something very important. Consider for example the Black Country construction 'I ay'. We could 'translate' this as 'I am not' or 'I'm not', but we would be missing out on the information that this form can also mean 'I have not', or 'I haven't', or, if we are a Scottish Standard English speaker, 'I've not'. We risk also biasing the reader and making an inadvertent judgement on the register which this construction is suited to if we choose the more colloquial contracted 'translation' 'I'm not' or 'I haven't'. Instead it is preferable to *explain* the construction:

I	ay [aɪeɪ]
First person subject pronoun	*be*NEG
or	
First person subject pronoun	*have*NEG

Morphology is arguably the most distinctive component of the Black Country and Birmingham linguistic systems. Many morphological structures (those of the auxiliary and modal verbs in particular) differ radically from those of Standard English, and some (especially in the

Black Country system) differ from any other variety of English spoken. This chapter gives first a description of the morphology and, to a lesser extent, the syntax of the dialect. It draws on existing research into the grammatical structure of the dialect to provide structure for adding present day empirical evidence from real-time data. We comment also on areas where linguists have overlooked certain features of the dialect's structure, and on certain features which they have pronounced extinct.

3.2 Numerals and Determiners

The numeric system of Black Country and Birmingham varieties is similar to that of Standard English. However Higgs (2004: 91) makes the point that the numeric systems and the definite determiner 'the' interact differently to the way they do in the standard variety. The numerals are found in utterances such as 'the one year, we went away for Christmas', or 'the one chap had his leg missing'. This construction is still in widespread use. The following examples show this clearly:

> 'they did eventually find out [someone's real name](.)the one(.)the one place they stopped was the curate(.)and when they got there he said Green'

> 'and I turned round the one day(.)and I said'
> (Asprey 2007: 106)

Higgs (2004: 91) also points to two related constructions using 'the' where the West Midlands standard does not. Thus constructions such as 'the women am the same', for an indefinite group of women, are found in his data, and Asprey's 2007 data. For example, an informant who remarks: 'I didn't want to put anything down too rude(.)kind of, like drunk, I might . . . I know the wife always says "peed".'

In a similar way, 'the' can occur with some proper nouns: 'He works up the Asda', for example, including names. Asprey (2007: 106) gives the following construction:

> A: 'Well I was led to believe as Florrie had the biggest child in Old Hill.'
> B: 'Well I was born in Netherton.'
> A: 'Well the Florrie's was about thirteen pound in weight.'

Tennant (1983: 39) also comments on what he calls the 'intrusive *the*' in Birmingham. He remarks that 'I was informed by a non-Brummy friend of mine that citizens of Birmingham had a habit of putting the definite article in front of the names of major roads, e.g. The Hagley Road, the Bristol Road, etc.'

An older construction is a variant of the definite determiner [ðə], which becomes [ð] before vowels, at least in the Black Country, though as yet there is no evidence to suggest its being used in Birmingham – thus [ðo:d] for West Midlands standard 'the old'. This form appears in Asprey's 2007 data from elderly informants; one talks of how he used to 'take the candle across [the yard] at night time(.)get on the toilet(.)break [ðais]', and another says 'I was in the pub [ðʊðədei](.)and my brother-law [brother-in-law] was late.'

One final difference is the use of 'a twothree' [ətu:θri:] to indicate 'a couple'; thus, 'a twothree weeks', for example. Asprey (2007: 107) hypothesises that this numeric determiner is undergoing age-related change, with all but the oldest speakers using [əkʊpləθri:] as a substitute. She gives an example:

'A term I used it's got to be [əkʊpləTri:] years ago now(.)it's raining like stair rods(.)and nobody knew what I meant(.)see the woman I'd said it to didn't know what stair rod was.'

This might be seen as a move towards a more standard form, but with the structure of the older form.

Trudgill (1999: 85) remarks that 'Many Non-standard Modern Dialects employ *them* or *they* rather than *those*.' Black Country and Birmingham varieties both have a system of distal and proximal determiners shown in Figure 3.1. Examination of the plural distal proves simple, since it differs in a purely binary fashion from that of Standard English.

Of Asprey's thirty-nine informants in the Black Country, 84.6 per cent reported hearing non-standard plural distal 'them', having been given the test sentence 'which apples do you want – them red ones or them green ones?' However, only 18 per cent of all informants reported using the form. This proved to be part of a pattern where the more recognised and obvious a form is to informants, the more they report not using it. During interview, for example, one informant revealed that

	Singular	Plural
Proximal	This book	These books
Distal	That book	Them books

Figure 3.1 Distal and Proximal Determiners (after Asprey 2007)

'I sometimes use "them", but I don't like it when I do', despite having reported that she never did. Examples from Asprey's 2007 data include:

> INF: 'You know them ones that are sort of like elasticated.'
> INF: 'But in them days my nan sent my mum to a home, for like single mothers.'
> INF: 'All them t-shirts.'

3.3 Nouns

Noun morphology in the Birmingham and Black Country varieties does not now differ from West Midlands Standard English as radically as does verb morphology. The *Survey of English Dialects* (*SED*) records [tuːɪəɹəgoɤ] for the standard phrase 'two years ago', showing the invariant plural form (Orton and Barry 1971: 764). This phenomenon is still observable at lower levels in Black Country and Birmingham varieties today. Though Rock (1974: 14) notes forms such as 'these cabbitch' for 'these cabbages', the construction now appears almost exclusively with a preceding numeral, usually with time and money references, the numeral bearing the semantic burden of plurality. Asprey (2007) gives the following example not directly related to a unit of measurement (weight, counting, mass etc), and since it relates to trousers, which must themselves be referred to in binary terms as a *pair*, it is ambiguous: 'He put two pair of trousers on.'

On the other hand, invariant plural in the Black Country was investigated by Asprey (2007) using test sentences which informants judged as possible or impossible. Ninety per cent of speakers who answered the question with the test sentence, 'It cost me about two pound', reported hearing such a construction, and 46 per cent reported using such a construction. One informant remarked tellingly at interview that she could not see what was wrong with the sentence, which might suggest that for some speakers at least the construction is below the level of consciousness. Other examples from the data include:

> INF: 'A couple of year later.'
> INF: 'Our babby was twelve-month old.'
> INF: 'I should have been married thirty-six year today; thirty-six year.'
> INF: 'Nearly forty-nine year this year.'
> INF: 'Twenty-five year in the March.'

The Midlands ending [n] (residual, for example, in Standard English 'oxen') is mentioned in older literature. Manley (1971) gives 'flen' [flɛn] for 'fleas', and [aʊzn] for 'houses', and Rock (1974: 14) working in Quarry Bank with informants aged seventy and over, gives 'housen', 'peasen', 'scorn' ('scores') and 'yearn'. By 2004, Higgs makes no mention of such a pluralising strategy. Thorne (2003: 76–7) reports on the various differences between Standard English and Birmingham English (BhamEng) in terms of nouns. He mentions that:

> A . . . morphological peculiarity of Brummagem speech is the way in which some plural nouns are often marked with an -en inflection. As Freeborn (1998: 105) points out, OE [Old English] plurals were marked with a variety of different inflections, <-as, -u, -ru, -a, 0an>, or with a zero inflection, or by a change of vowel. . . . The OE plural of <ċild> was <ċildru>, which became Middle English <childre> or <childer>. In one dialect childer was given an additional -en suffix – childeren – which has become the Standard English children. A few other examples of this exist in the present day Standard English plural doems of ox (oxen) and brother (brethren).

Brummie seems unique, he continues, in that – for older speakers at least – 'housen' is still in use as the plural form of 'house'. He does not report any instances from his own data, however, and does not make explicit the fact that other dialects also used the feature, as an Essex ballad *Them Harnted Housen* clearly shows:

> Goo' mornin', sir, you minter say you bought them housen there,
> An' you're a-go'n ter live in one ? Well, that'll make 'em stare.
> Them housen sir, is harnted, an' was when I's a lad,
> An' anyone as sleep there, sir, is sartin to be had.
> (Benham: 1890)

3.4 Pronouns

Differing from a conventional pronominal system 'issun' meaning 'his' and 'ern' meaning 'hers' is used in lieu of the Standard English possessive cases which are redolent of the Black Country and Birmingham.

3.4.1 Subject Pronouns

The third person female singular subject pronoun is usually [əː] rather than [ʃiː] among those at the local end of the linguistic continuum. For example (Asprey 2007: 109):

> INF: 'Her came over.'
> INF: 'And her didn't understand what they meant by adjacent.'

This is a historically western Midlands usage, shown in the display map of McIntosh et al. (1986: item map 4).

The use of subject 'thee' [ði] or 'thou' [ðaʊ] for second person singular is considered by Trudgill and Chambers (1991: 8) to be a feature of 'traditional dialects'. Once again, the line between the traditional and the new is blurred; the retention of this pronoun in the undeniably urban dialect of Sheffield, for example, belies this contention. The pronoun 'you' has been in use in the Black Country as the second person plural subject form for many years, and the paradigm is now being levelled to 'you' for both singular and plural forms. Higgs (2004) finds only one example of 'thou' or 'thee' usage in his sample, as does Asprey 2007. She cites an eighty year-old informant:

> 'If I go down the club or I'm playing bowls with [eərəwɒn] [someone] [aːbɪnjə] mate?(.)Oh I'm alright(.)[ði dɤsnt lʊk tə bæd]".'
> (Asprey 2007: 109)

Rock (1974: 14) discusses the form and its distribution in the Black Country. Her speakers, aged seventy and over, in Quarry Bank give enough instances for her to be able to explain that 'the second person singular form *thee* . . . is used when conversing with a friend, both in subjective forms such as "*hie thee off*", and as the object: "*what I'm a-tryin' to tell thee, my wench . . .*". The corresponding possessive form is *thy*, with the disjunctive *thine*.'

3.4.2 Object Pronouns

Second person object pronoun

Thorne (2003: 77) reports that '*yous* [alternative spelling is *youse*] [juːz] is the second person plural pronoun in the . . . subject, direct object and indirect object forms'. There is well-documented evidence of 'yous' as being found in Hiberno-English and Liverpool English, Liverpool being a city which, like Birmingham, has a large population of first, second and third generation Irish immigrants. It is possible that the distinction between *tú* (second person singular) and *sibh* (second person plural) in Irish may have contributed to this distinction arising in the Celtic countries and in cities with large immigrant Irish populations, though Wales (1996: 73) points out that:

> many dialects and varieties of English seem to find a distinction extremely
> useful between a single addressee and more than one . . . This fact is rarely
> acknowledged by contemporary grammarians, if at all: for example, there is

heard yous(e) in Dublin and northern English from Liverpool to Glasgow, and also northern American English, with a noun plural morpheme <s> by analogy (c.f. general Hiberno-English/ Newfoundland *yiz*); this is dubbed a 'low-prestige' form by Quirk et al. (1985: 6.12) in a footnote.

Many Creoles, such as Tok Pisin, have created such a two-way distinction for themselves, namely *yu* versus *yu tupela*. Hogg (2000) agrees that:

> because of long-term change in the English pronominal system, the standard language has lost a critical element of the system, namely the ability to distinguish singular and plural forms of the second person pronoun: for both we have to use *you*. What happens in non-standard dialects? If we leave aside those dialects which still cling on to *thou*, which are in any case fast disappearing, what we find is rather interesting. Many many dialects have created new pronouns: *you all, y'all, yiz, youse, youse yins, y'uns, you guys, you lot.* None of these have become standard, although it might be that in standard American *you guys* may be nearest to achieving that status. Such forms have, of course, arisen precisely because the standard language is inadequate in this core area.

There is plentiful written web-based evidence for this form existing in Birmingham speech. Birmingham: It's Not Shit was a local website which, among others things, hosted a forum for people wishing to discuss the history and language of Birmingham, and organised the UK-wide Talk Like A Brummie Day every year. It contained some good examples:

> Tumblr is what the geek world calls a 'microblogging' platform – which kind of means that it tries to make it easy for you to blog (well, share internet stuff anyway) . . . What this has got to do with youse is that . . . it's a very cool and easy way to get into blogging if you so fancy. (Bounds 2007)

Similarly, posting on a piano players' forum about a music video he has uploaded, user *dave brum* remarked 'youse will all get to see my face – how cool is that!!' (UK Piano Page Piano Discussion Forums 2009).

3.4.3 First Person Singular Object Pronoun

Rock (1974: 14) makes the point that 'us', which represents in Standard English the second person plural object form, is 'rarely used in its normal plural sense, [but] is widely used in such phrases as "come and find us" to mean "me", and "giz", which is a shortened form of "give it us'". This is the case for many speakers, both young and old, within my sample. Giving his alternative for the notion 'to throw', one informant remarks 'I'd say chuck us that . . . chuck that to me.' Though this is by no means restricted to Birmingham and the Black Country local varieties (see for example Snell 2007), it is nevertheless part of the local system.

The system of object pronouns in the Black Country shows the use of 'we' where West Midlands Standard English has 'us'. Asprey (2007: 110) gives the example of an informant remarking that the people she met on her holidays last year annoyed her because 'they used to call we Brummies'. She also gives the following exchange:

> 'Did you see a lot of people like this who were laying it on with a trowel [their accent] and pretending to be Black Country?'
> 'Yeah yeah well yeah cause I thought which is like see they don't(.)to me they don't do we no favours(.)I mean cause they're not natural(.)they're not natural(.)it's just put on.'

Asprey 2007 suggests that many researchers are too quick to suggest that a form is extinct, basing such conclusions on their own small datasets. Higgs (2004: 84) comments on this with regard to the use of 'we' as object pronoun, remarking that 'personally, I have never heard this use in Black Country dialect, and it would seem likely that, like th-pronouns, it has virtually disappeared'. It may be, however, that the phenomenon is one from the northern Black Country, since Higgs only decided to investigate it having read the 1975 bible translation by Kate Fletcher (who grew up in Bilston). If informants in the south of the Black Country were using 'we' for third person possessive as well as subject pronoun, it might mean that the use of 'we' for object pronoun would have meant confusing syncretism within the pronominal paradigm, though there is evidence from nineteenth-century dialect poetry for 'we' as possessive pronoun having existed in Bilston speech too, which muddies the water concerning these particular features.

Certainly, Asprey (2007) reports that informants as far south as Dudley claim to have heard the use of 'we' as object pronoun construction, which undermines Higgs's theory that that particular construction is extinct. The example below from a Dudley born informant is a good one, since she deliberately emphasised her allusion to the pronominal choice, rather than the verb morphology: 'I like erm we had it gid **we**. I can hear people(.)I can hear family saying that.' (Asprey 2007: 110).

3.4.4 Possessive Pronouns

Thorne reports that the older possessive pronominal system in Birmingham displays levelling through the paradigm. There appears to be no evidence of such levelling in Old English (OE); Sweet (1995: 22) gives the possessive pronoun paradigm in OE as:

1st person singular	mīn
2nd person singular	Þīn
3rd person singular masculine	his
3rd person singular feminine	hi(e)re
3rd person plural (all numbers)	hi(e)ra

Fisiak (1968: 86) gives the West Midlands Middle English paradigm as:

1st person singular	mīn
2nd person singular	Þīn
3rd person singular masculine	his
3rd person singular feminine	hire, here, hir, her
	heore, here, hyr, her, hor, hure, hyr, hire, Þeir
All plural forms (early Middle English)	
1st person plural	oures
2nd person plural	youres
3rd person plural (late Middle English)	hires, heres

But Fisiak remarks crucially that 'except in the North, one can also find in Middle English the second possessive case in -*en*, analogically created after the forms in -*n* (*mīn*, *Þīn*), as *hisen*, *ouren*, *theiren*, etc. These forms can be met in some British and American dialects today.' (1968: 88).

Tennant (1982) gives the following definitions which back this evidence and suggest that some of these forms are still in operation:

Ern – belonging to her, e.g. 'it's ern', meaning 'This is her property'. Yawn – belonging to you, as in 'is this'n yawn?' – 'No, it's isn' meaning 'Does this belong to you? No, it belongs to him'.

Investigating in Cradley Heath in the south of the Black Country in the early 1970s, Manley reports that the possessive pronominal system runs as follows:

1st person sg.	mine [maɪn]
2nd person sg.	thine [ðaɪn]
3rd person sg.	izen [ɪzn] / 'erzens / shezens [ɜːzənz] / [ʃiːzənz]
1st person pl.	ourn [aʁən]
2nd person pl.	yourn [joʁən]
3rd person pl.	theirn [ðɛːrən]

Figure 3.2 Black Country Possessive Pronouns (after Manley 1971)

Orton and Barry (1971: 1,061) record [joʁən], rather than [ðaɪn] in the *SED* material, suggesting that syncretism within the pronominal system has been present for many decades, and showing also that forms related to 'thee' were already less common. Asprey's own observations confirm that [joʁən~jɔːn] is still in use. In the same way, the third person singular female pronoun still exists, though it is now reduced to [ɜːn]. Rock (1974: 14) documents this change among her speakers in Quarry Bank (who are of an age with Manley's informants in Cradley Heath), remarking that 'the disjunctive form is "hers'n" or "hern"'. Asprey's informants (2007: 112) give an example of this form:

'Pam's got all [ɜːn ei ja] Pam?'
'What [mɪ] teeth?'

Possessive Pronouns
Bartlett (1886) exemplifies the use of 'we' as the plural possessive pronoun in the plural form in his dialect poetry: 'Er's a knittin' soo's ter get we grub, poor wench.' Rock (1974: 14) gives sentences from her informants which include:

we   work
our Poss Prn Pl   work

as well as 'on we own', and 'we'd had it all we lives'. Manley too gives the utterance 'we'm on we own' (1971: 59). It is inappropriate to speculate about its levels of use here, just as it was to speculate about use of 'we' as an object pronoun. More data are needed to do so.

Reflexive Pronouns and the 'Personal Dative'

Trudgill and Chambers (1991: 8) remark that 'many non-standard dialects of English have a regularised system of reflexive pronouns in which all forms are based on the possessive pronouns'. The Black Country relative pronoun paradigm is a good example of this. Standard English has a system of reflexive pronouns which work by adding '-self' to the possessive form of the pronoun, with the exception of 'himself' and 'themselves' which are formed using the object pronoun as the base morpheme. Black Country and Birmingham, like many other varieties, do not contain this inconsistency. Asprey (2007: 112) gives a good example of this when discussing politics with an informant: 'These other parties [əv] got to look at theirselves [eɪ] they?'.

The normal pronouns used at the local end of the continuum are 'hisself' and 'theirselves'. Of Asprey's 2007 informants, 82 per cent reported hearing 'hisself' in their local area when given the test sentence 'I told him he'd have to go hisself', but only 38 per cent reported actually using it.

What Higgs (2004) terms the 'personal dative' is investigated primarily to ascertain levels of usage. According to Trudgill and Chambers (1991: 10), such structures appear to 'contravene the syntactic rules concerning reflexives that are found in most other English dialects'. There was formerly a complete paradigm for this structure; utterances such as 'he washed him', 'we bought us one' were in widespread use in the Black Country (see Rock 1974: 14). Christian (1991: 11) reports on the structure as it exists in Appalachian English. She explains that 'in English, when the same referent is mentioned twice within a clause, the second occurrence typically takes on a reflexive form, that is, a form with -self . . . In some varieties of English, it is possible to use a non-reflexive pronoun ('you', 'me' and so on) in certain cases for the second occurrence of a single referent within the same clause.' In the Black Country and Birmingham local varieties, utterances such 'I shall have to get me one of them' are perfectly grammatical. For example, from Asprey's data (2007: 113) the feature appears to be in common usage, with one informant stating: 'This one day I'd been [wɜːkɪnmɪˈjɛdɒf](.) and I had me a cup of tea.'

This grammatical element is also displayed in the following construction:

INF: 'I couldn't believe it; I can't get me hat off.'
(Asprey 2007: 113)

3.4.5 Relative Pronouns

The two relative pronouns discussed earlier as a result of their being included in the list of sentences which informants were presented with were 'what' and 'as'. Together with zero marker Ø, all are all in evidence in the Black Country today. Higgs (2004: 86) finds in his own data that 'as' 'occurred in older peoples' samples', whereas 'what' 'occurred through-out the age range'. The *SED* (Orton and Barry 1971: 1,072) records the phrase 'the man as his uncle got drownded' for West Midlands Standard English 'the man whose uncle was drowned'. Though relative, 'what' is also attested in the 1950s by fieldworkers on the *SED*, and as far back as 1886 in the dialect poetry of F. R. Bartlett:

> An' wuss luck, ah'm the feyther
> O' that lad wot laertly died . . .
> In the snow wot were a-lyin',
> Moor'n a foot deep on the ground!

'What' is in common use today in both Birmingham and the Black Country varieties and is also a feature which appears more widely across the UK. Tape-recorded interviews conducted in 2001 (Asprey 2001) show younger speakers using only 'what' as a relativiser, and not 'as', which would give the sentence 'the man whats uncle got drownded'. This variation in relative pronoun may therefore represent a change in progress. Informants in Asprey (2007) were given two target sentences to comment on:

1. The chap what fixed my car last week was ever so rude to me.
2. Which chap? – The chap as owns the brown dog.

Of these informants, 61.5 per cent had heard the target 'what' for the relative pronoun with an inanimate object. Only 7.7 per cent said that they would use the form ($n=3$). Of the fifteen informants who reported never having heard the form, eleven were forty years old and over. Other examples from the data include:

INF: 'Because they've got languages what he day do.'
INF: 'I talk more Black Country than what she does and she's from the Black Country.'

3.5 Adjectives and Adverbs

Rock (1974: 15) discusses adjectives which have the [ən] suffix such as 'leaden', 'brassen' and 'erden' hessian). Beach (1998) points out that the Glynne Arms at Himley – a public house which has partly sunk into a poorly capped mine shaft – is still known not only as the Crooked House, but as the Siden House, 'siden' meaning 'out of perpendicular, out of true'.

Thorne (2003: 76) describes adjectival forms in use in Birmingham which end with the OE suffix -en. He reports that 'boughten cake' is different to home-made cake. Though Thorne gives no current examples from his own data, he reports on stock phrases which are in use by older people, such as having 'the brassen skimmer rubbed over your face' as a common phrase meaning a person who is impudent or audacious.

Comparative adjectives are found as double comparatives with the comparative 'more' as well as suffixation relatively frequently. Asprey (2007) cites a nineteen year-old informant as saying 'Lee's from Cannock(.)I can tell(.)cause he speaks more posher', and from another informant, 'No. You're from somewhere more classier like Castle Vale.' Howarth (1988: 12), working in Pleck (central Walsall) just outside the Black Country, reports the use of [wʊsa] for Standard English 'worse', and [bɛtərə] for 'better'. 'All the while' is common as a compound adverb in the area.

There is also the tendency for adjectives and adverbs to appear with an identical form so that adverbs do not have a -ly suffix. In this way, 'he ate slow', 'I day do bad', and 'they got there really quick' are all acceptable and common constructions in the Black Country local variety. They do not seem subject to scrutiny by speakers. Asprey gives a conversation with a young student vehemently opposed to the local speech variety; indeed, much of her interview was devoted to this topic, yet even she remarks during this:

EA: 'So you would change where you came from(.)would you change where you came from?'
INF: 'It's not necessarily the place(.)like the place itself(.)it's just the accent(.) just the accent(.)and it makes it worse at Uni cause like all the people you hang around with(.)at home(.)but like(.)here it's like accentuated cause everyone speaks *completely different.*'
(Asprey 2007: 116)

Asprey's informants also show that for some speakers it is possible to use local forms to form adverbs used without premodification with other intensifiers (bearing in mind also that the standard 'heavily' was actually part of the notion phrase given on the page):

> EA: 'What would you say for the weather?'
> INF: 'To rain *heavy*(.)shaft it down.'

The same informant gives another example of this:

> INF: 'You can't take things *serious* at work.'
> (Asprey 2007: 117)

Further evidence of the neutralisation of a distinction between adverb and adjective is found in the data:

> INF: 'They do really good though, don't they?'
> INF: 'Talking really broad.'
> INF: 'Everybody talks different.'

3.6 Prepositions

Prepositional usage within the Black Country is different from that of West Midlands Standard English. Many of the Black Country examples given in Asprey (2007) match exactly those given by Thorne (2003: 68) relating to Birmingham. Among these include use of 'up' for 'to', the use of 'off' for 'from', and the use of 'on' for 'of'. Thorne also mentions the use of 'of a' in place of Standard English 'on', 'in', and 'at'. Thus he gives 'they used to come in of a Christmas morning, whoever woke first', 'up early of a mornin', do all 'er 'ousework', and 'and 'e used ter stop at all the pubs but 'e could bring 'im 'ome of a night even if 'e was kaylied [drunk]'. This is also found in the Black Country quite regularly. In this grammatical category then, Birmingham and Black Country varieties appear identical.

Informants in Asprey 2007 are often clearly aware of the differences between the local and supralocal varieties:

> But something I(.)I've never said myself – but working where I work cause I'm suddenly working with people from all round the Black Country – is that they say not(.)I'm going to the loo(.)I'm going on the loo.'

The Dudley edition of the *Express and Star* ran a humorous article in 1981 discussing a theme, still under consideration today, that teachers were requesting tuition to help them understand the local

Standard English	Black Country English	Example
from	off	I got a present off my Mum.
to	up	INF: 'n when I went to(.)er up Dudley on the market.'
to	on	I'm going on the loo.
to	down	I'm going down the pub.
of	on	INF: 'You've been banned from half the pubs [eɪja] [Laughs] you've been banned from half on [əm].'
Verb + *with*	Verb + of	INF: 'Spitting [ə] rain.'
with	of	The plate was that high of pancakes.
afterwards	after	INF: 'We went through a fad of going up there on a Saturday night(.)either before or without going to a club or something after.'
at + Ø	on a/the	INF: 'If [juːm] out on a night time.'
in	at	INF: 'That was er when I lived at Langley.'

Figure 3.3 The Prepositional System in the Black Country

Black Country variety. The article went to press with the headline 'Teachers need lessons . . . off Aynuk'. It is significant that an informant in Figure 3.3 revises her utterance to choose the local preposition since it suggests that there is no stigma attached, at least, to the use of locative 'up' for 'to'. It is not possible that she corrected for locative accuracy – she lived at the top of the largest hill in Dudley, and the market was a long way downhill.

Rock (1974: 15) reports the absence of 'of' in complex prepositions like 'a lot of'. This gives sentences like 'a lot odd jobs'. This construction does not appear in our data.

Examples of prepositional usage difference across the data include:

INF: 'She'd go the butchers.'
INF: 'Out my head.'
INF: 'Out the library.'
INF: 'We got back on a night.'

Standard English	Black Country English	Example
otherwise	else	Hold still, else you'll have to go up the hospital.
so that	so as	It got so as you couldn't move for rubbish.
but	only	'I'm sorry I'm late, only I fell over.' (Rock, 1974: 15)
except	only	'You never had a cup of tea, only when it was tea time.' (Rock, 1974: 15)
unless	without	'They won't come in, without you give them a cup of tea.' (Rock, 1974: 15)

Figure 3.4 The Conjunction System in the Black Country

3.7 Conjunctions

Figure 3.4 outlines differences again between West Midlands standard and Black Country and Birmingham conjunction use. Like prepositional usage, conjunction use differs from the standard, and there are large-scale similarities between Birmingham and the Black Country.

3.8 Main Verb Systems in Birmingham and the Black Country: Regularisation

The main verb system in Birmingham and the Black Country mostly differs from the standard in the formation of the past tense and past participle. Many verbs are regularised across the paradigm at the past tense form, and others regularised at the past participial form. There may also be complete levelling at the present tense form. Asprey (2007: 121) gives the following examples from her data in the Black Country which display many of these strategies. The strategies not displayed, but nevertheless in evidence in Asprey's data, are those of using the weak suffix -ed rather than the rarer strong verb pattern found among certain verbs in Standard English, thus giving forms like 'I [sɪd] him yesterday'. Thorne in Birmingham (2003: 69–70) gives examples of regularisation using weak suffixes such as 'I knowed him a long time ago' and 'I've knowed 'er since 'er was a nipper'. He gives examples of regularisation to the past participial form such as 'Well, a chap [sɪn] me 'avin' a fight in the street' and 'The reason they done that was . . .'. He also gives the example 'If I'd 'ave give up my 'ome I couldn't take anything of my own with me.' The only strategy not attested in Birmingham, as it is in the

Present	Past	Past participle
come	come	come
INF: 'Grandad (.)went in the army, did seven years in India, come back, still no work.'		
drink	drunk	drunk
INF: 'We was surprised, that's why we drunk it.'		
take	took	took
INF: 'What, you've just took drugs – no, I was drunk.' INF: 'They have all their bits took out.'		
write	wrote	wrote
INF: 'I've wrote "trousers" but it's [tɹaːzəz].' INF: 'I've wrote about music.'		
swear	swore	swore
INF: 'Yeah, cause he [woɤ] swear(.)he's never swore a day in his life.'		

Figure 3.5 Main Verb Systems in Birmingham and The Black Country: Regularisation

Black Country, is the use of ablaut. It is entirely likely that this has happened because these formations are now so restricted in use, and that further data collection may reveal their presence in Birmingham.

3.8.1 Main Verb Morphology: Strong Verbs for Standard English Weak Verbs

Standard English weak verbs which are strong in Black Country English were investigated by Asprey (2007) by means of a test sentence. This is the use of ablaut as a past marking strategy where Standard English uses suffixation. For example, one would hear 'puck' for StEng 'picked', and 'squoze' for StEng 'squeezed':

INF: 'He squoze himself into like a little Mini.'

Sometimes heard is a regularisation or simplification of mixed verbs, for example, 'brung' for StEng 'brought'. Informants were given the sentence 'They gave me a choice, so I puck the cheapest.' (In retrospect, it would have been more authentic to also employ the more frequent strategy of regularisation of 'give' in the test sentence; thus, 'They gid me a choice . . .'). Fifty-six per cent of informants had heard the structure, but only 13 per cent said they would use the structure themselves. One sixty-nine year-old informant remarked 'It's about fifty years since I heard "puck" in conversation.' Conversely, another informant aged twenty-one remarked, 'I would use that.'

There is a tendency to produce weak past tense forms at the local end of the variety continuum for Standard English strong verbs. It means that Manley (1971: 47–8) finds the paradigm shown in Figure 3.6 for the verb 'give'. Other verbs, including 'see', also behave in this way (though [sɪd] is found alongside its alternative [sɪn], which can also be used for both past tense and past participle, and again, regardless of number). Thus, 'You'd(.)leg it)(.)before they [sɪnjəfæɪs]'; but, also from the same informant at the same interview, 'If you've [sɪd] like(.)the music video to it is(.)[ðɛɪm] all drunk in it(.)like.'

> These two examples do seem to suggest that [sɪn] represents past tense, and [sɪd] participial usage. Although these weak forms are noted by Manley, as yet no sociolinguistic work on their distribution and social significance has been undertaken.

One informant gave another instance of this Black Country past participle form for the past tense: 'I never [sɪn] a dog or cat.'

Manley's paradigm for 'give' (Figure 3.6) shows that, with the removal of the second person distinction from the paradigm, there is now levelling at [gɪd] throughout the past tense and past participle, as demonstrated by one informant's description of his alternative for the verb 'hit': '[iː sɪd] somebody Saturday night [zero relativiser] [gɪd] somebody a right towelling'.

Another gave an account of specifically arranging a teaching session on Black Country language for his English for Speakers of Other Languages (ESOL) students:

> I became very conscious about what I'm saying cause they started saying 'we can't understand people round here!' The one chap was from Iraq and er(.)he says he got on a bus(.)and the bus driver had said something back to him(.)'da' or something(.)I said he's saying 'ta' cause you've [gɪd] him the money.

3.8.2 Levelling of Weak Verbs across the Time Distinctions

To take this analysis further, in Black Country English there can be a lack of distinction between past tense and past participle, with the form for both either being the standard past form or the standard past participle. Verbs with a three-way distinction between present, past and the

Present tense	Past tense	Past participle
ɒ gɪz/giː	ɒ gɪd	gɪd
ði: gɪst	ði: gɪdst	gɪd
i: ɜ: ɪt gɪz	i: ɜ: ɪt gɪd	gɪd
wi: gɪən	wi: gɪd	gɪd
jɔʏ gɪən	jɔʏ gɪd	gɪd
ðeɪ gɪən	ðeɪ gɪd	gɪd

Figure 3.6 Past Tense Verb Paradigm: 'give' (after Manley 1971)

past participle can also have the same forms, this time the standard past form. Examples of both strategies are given in Figure 3.6.

Verb Morphology: -s Marking

Higgs (2004) finds a small amount of evidence for the continuing existence of the -s present tense marker on main verbs (not just in the 'narrative tense', where they appear extremely frequently among all age groups with the verbs 'say' and 'go'). Asprey's data (2007: 121) shows examples from informants over seventy, including an informant asked about the word for 'ears' who remarked, 'lugs(.)I [kɔːlzəm](.)lugholes', and an informant who claimed that 'to work hard(.)you [græfs]' and 'I always [kɔːlz] it the living room.' Trudgill (1990: 102) remarks that this is found in 'very many western and northern dialects . . . in Traditional and Modern dialect alike'. Asprey suggests that the feature is recessive and restricted to older speakers within the south of the Black Country. One final point is the use of the -s inflection on the 'narrative tense' form which speakers had been asked to comment on. In Cradley Heath, an informant from the 71+ age group reported that she used the construction herself, rereading it to me with the -s inflection added: 'He comes in here last night to see me.' There is no evidence of this morpheme still occurring in Birmingham dialect, though again, there is less data available concerning Birmingham.

3.8.3 Main Verb Conjugation Across Time

Trudgill (1990: 102) remarks that:

> It is also possible to find Traditional Dialects in which the older plural forms in -en are retained, as in we putten, they cutten = 'we put, they cut'. These are particularly common in the Staffordshire dialect area.

Wakelin (1972: 120–1) explains that:

> in OE, the plural usually ended in -aþ, ME -eth, but in Modern Standard English the plural inflection is completely lost and there is no ending. In the dialects, any trace of -eth endings . . . seems to have vanished completely . . . but a geographically more restricted feature still present is the ending -(e)n, which already appears in the ME Midland dialects, and is usually explained as having originated in the present subjunctive form.

These forms are attested in Manley (1971), and even in Higgs (2004). Thus, the paradigm for 'know', according to Manley, runs:

I know [noʁ(z)]
Thee [noʁst]
He/she/it [noʁz]
We you they [noʁən]

Again, there is the possibility of the [z] morpheme in first person singular, and one sees quite clearly the -en form which, by 2004, Higgs (62) says is 'an ancient form which has all but disappeared'. Asprey's data (2007: 123) have two informants who still use this form. B gives the following example (in line four) discussing the birth weight of A, a record in his village at the time:

A 'Fourteen and half pound.'
B 'Ooh [joʊ wɒn] [*be*Neg Past]?'
A 'When I were born.'
B 'Ooh [joʊ wən] [*be*Affirm Past] a [bɪgən].'

And again:

A 'I mean I used to live in a back-to-front house [i.e. not a through house].'
B 'Yeah, that's what these [wəɹn](.)back to front.'

3.8.4 Lack of Verb Distinctions

Finally, there is the lack of semantic distinction between 'lend' and 'borrow', 'lend' being the preferred form for both. Similarly there is the collapse of 'teach' and 'learn'; 'learn' is the preferred form for both. This cuts across all age groups, though it is frowned upon, and parents will correct their children if they do this. One informant remarks to another when the interviewer suggests the word 'wammal' for 'dog' (he having forgotten that he knew the word): 'Ooh – I never thought about that one, eh? Her's learned us [sʊmət] today.' (Asprey 2007: 123).

Support Verb Morphology

The system of support verb morphology in the neighbouring Black Country is somewhat further removed from Standard English than that of Birmingham English, though the two varieties have much in common in this morphological category. The formation of present tense declarative 'be' is a good example of the latter. Thorne (2003: 71) explains that:

> Like Black Country speakers, Brummies occasionally produce 'bin' rather than 'are' or the third person plural, as in this example from an anonymous inscription reproduced in Palmer (1976: 7): 'Man, it behoves thee oft to have in minde/ That thou dealest with the hand that shalt thou find:/ Children bin slothful, and wives bin unkind,/ Executors bin covetous and keep all they find.

It it in fact the case that in the Black Country a relict paradigm is occasionally heard which goes far beyond use of 'bin' in third person plural form only.

'Be' present tense affirmative	'Be' present tense negative
I am	ɒ bɪn
You are	ðɪ bɪst
He/she/it is	iː ɜː ɪt ɪz
We are	wiː bɪn
You are	joʊ bɪn
They are	ðeɪ bɪn

Figure 3.7 Present Tense Verb Paradigm: 'be'

Thorne does not provide evidence of this in his examination of the Birmingham data, which indicates that this form may indeed be now restricted to the older generation and to the third person plural. However, his contention that 'Ow bist yer [aʊ bɪst jə]' occurs in the Black Country is unlikely in the extreme. [bɪst] nearly always collocates with [ðɪ], and [bɪn] with [joʊ].

Examining the former provides a good introduction to the structure of the latter. Asprey (2007) collates research across the years to explain that auxiliaries and modal verbs in the Black Country use the unusual strategy of ablaut to mark negation, and that this system is still in common use across the generations. Use of Manley's 1971 study in Cradley Heath in the southern Black Country, compared with Asprey's 2007 data, shows that the system has only changed over time in terms of the loss of 'thee' as second person singular pronoun.

Present tense negative (older)	Present tense negative (newer)
ɒɪ æn → eɪ	ɒɪ æv → eɪ
ði: æst → æsnt	joʊ æv → eɪ
i: ɜ: ɪt æz → eɪ	i: ɜ: ɪt æz → eɪ
wi: æn → eɪ	wi: æv → eɪ
joʊ æn → eɪ	joʊ æv → eɪ
ðeɪ æn → eɪ	ðeɪ æv → eɪ

Figure 3.8 Auxiliary Verb 'have': Negative Forms (after Asprey 2007 and Manley 1971)

Birmingham English, in contrast, retains a negative particle -nt in the support verb system, so that the paradigm for 'have' would run as follows in the present tense:

This phenomenon occurs in the Black Country with several other verb forms, including the main verb 'do' and operator 'do' in both the past and present tense.

Present tense negative
ɒɪ æv → eɪnt
joʊ æv → eɪ eɪnt
i: ɜ: ɪt æz → eɪnt
wi: æv → eɪnt
joʊ æv → eɪnt
ðeɪ æv → eɪnt

Figure 3.9 Present Tense Verb Paradigm 'have'

Past tense negative (Manley 1971)	Past tense negative (Asprey 2007)	Birmingham English (various sources)
ɒ deɪ	ɒ deɪ	ɒ deɪnt
ði: dɪsnt	joʏ deɪ	joʏ deɪnt
i: ɜ: ɪt deɪ	i: ɜ: ɪt deɪ	i: ɜ: ɪt deɪnt
wi: deɪ	wi: deɪ	wi: deɪnt
joʏ deɪ	joʏ deɪ	ju:z deɪnt/ joʏ deɪnt
ðeɪ deɪ	ðeɪ deɪ	ðeɪ deɪnt

Figure 3.10 Past Tense Negative Verb Paradigm: 'have'

	Past tense negative BC English (Asprey 2007)	Birmingham English (various sources)
'Have' pres neg 'Be' pres neg	ai eɪ	ai ɪnt
'Be' past neg	ai wɔ:	ai wɔ:nt
'Do' past neg	ai deɪ	ai deɪnt
'Do' past neg + qu inversion	deɪ jə	deɪntʃa/ deɪnja

Figure 3.11 Past Tense Negative Verb Paradigms: 'have', 'be', 'do'

Manley (1971) and Asprey (2007) again compare the negative paradigm of the verb in the past tense form across time in Figure 3.10. The only difference in their data is the loss of 'thee' as second singular object and subject pronoun, resulting in complete levelling of the paradigm at [deɪ]. This time, however, we have also included the paradigm for Birmingham English.

Birmingham English support morphology appears to be one step closer to Standard English, then, in that most verbs concerned contain a negative particle. Thus Tennant (1982) gives us 'yow in't' (for 'you haven't' and 'you aren't'), 'carntcha' (for 'can't you'), 'worn't' (for 'was not'/'were not'), 'dain't' (for 'didn't') and 'dainya' and 'daintcha' (for 'didn't you'). This last example, with its two possible variants, may provide a clue to the development of Black Country forms, which ironically, despite the iconic status accorded to them by speakers of the BC variety, may be newer than those of BhamEng. Figure 3.11 shows the differences between BC and BhamEng, comparing these forms with BC forms – for example, INF: 'I [deɪntˀ] do nothing'.

Second person plural forms in Birmingham still do not have enough written about them for it to be concluded that forms like [juːz deɪnt] actually exist; it seems likely that the pronoun can indeed exist with past tense [deɪnt] following it, but this has yet to be confirmed in fieldwork.

The most striking difference from West Midlands Standard English regarding conjugation of verbs concerns what is commonly known as operator 'do' (that is, 'do' used for negatives, interrogatives and emphasis) as well as modal and auxiliary verbs. Semi-modals also have a different structure, and some follow different syntactic patterns. The situation in the Black Country is extremely complex and confusing. Although the affirmative forms may also differ, the paradigms differ most noticeably from West Midlands Standard English in their negated forms.

Second person singular forms which appear with 'thee', based on Old English 'beōn', which take -st endings, are still in the speech and/ or receptive knowledge of the oldest speakers in Asprey's sample; for instance, 'It's ever so wet; you bay going out in this, bist?' In the same way, older speakers, both of them in the 71 + age group, give 'How bist?' as a greeting form for 'How are you?' One informant later explained at interview was the more likely form to accompany the negative 'bay' as a tag. Another informant in the 71 + group remarked that it was 'more likely to be "bin ya" in this century'.

> That's what they say(.)that round about Cradley was Old English actu-
> ally er(.)'bist' and 'bin'. We don't hear 'bist' much these days. We *used* to(.)
> Cradley Heath you still will(.)oh yes(.)'thou bist'(.)but not here so much.

Leaving aside this change in progress from 'thee' to 'you', there are still a myriad forms which seem at first sight to be in free variation. It is likely that 'bist' functions as a lexicalised marker of 'Blackcountryness'; this is evinced in spoof websites such as Winders 2007, the Black Country variety version of Microsoft Windows.

Curiously, it also shows that whoever wrote the spoof version is not a native speaker of Black Country, and is not as familiar with the variety as many in the region. The sentence 'Aer Kid am bostin' at 'elpin . . .' shows this, since to use 'am' for third person singular 'be' is incorrect ('is' is the correct form).

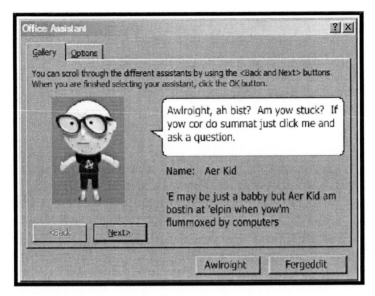

Figure 3.12 Black Country Microsoft Winders Assistant

3.8.5 Operator 'do': Affirmative and Negative

Operator 'do' is discussed by Manley (1971: 44–5). Again, she gives the older forms which show both the influence of the dual second person subject pronoun system, and that of Midlands verb ending -n.

The present tense of the verb does not mark negation in the way most Englishes do. There is no negative element attached to the verb: -n't, not, -na, -nae. Black Country local variety speakers mark negation by

Present tense affirmative	Past tense affirmative	Future time reference affirmative
ɒ dʌz /ɒ dʌn (emphatic)	ɒ dɪd	ɒ ʃɒn dɪə ~ ɒɪ ʃl dɪə
ði: dʌst	ði: dɪdst/dɪst	
i: ɜ: ɪt dʌz	i: ɜ: ɪt dɪd	
wi: dʌn	wi: dɪd	
jɒʏ dʌn	jɒʏ dɪd	
ðeɪ dʌn	ðeɪ dɪd	

Figure 3.13 Affirmative Paradigm 'do' (after Manley 1971)

Present tense negative	Past tense negative	Future time reference negative
ɒ doɣ	ɒ deɪ	ɒ ʃɒ: dɪə, ɒ oɣ dɪə
ði: dʌsnt	ði: dɪsnt	
i: ɜ: ɪt doɣ	i: ɜ: ɪt deɪ	
wi: doɣ	wi: deɪ	
joɣ doɣ	joɣ deɪ	
ðeɪ doɣ	ðeɪ deɪ	

Figure 3.14 Negative Paradigm 'do' (after Manley 1971)

mutation of the root vowel. The past tense paradigm, with the exception of the second person singular, also marks negation using sound mutation rather than a copula. Figure 3.14 shows the loss of the negative copula in both the present and past negative paradigm. The forms [doɣ] and [deɪ] have no negative particle attached to them. Instead, verb negation in the present paradigm is marked by a series of sound mutations. The past tense paradigm, with the exception of the second person singular, also marks negation using sound mutation rather than a copula.

Since the decline of 'thee' and 'thou', the Black Country forms of *do*Neg Past and *do*Neg Present are respectively [deɪ] and [doɣ] throughout the paradigms. This also applies to the use of 'do' as a main verb, though there is a continuum of more to less Black Country, with some 'compromise' possibilities lying between the Black Country and the West Midlands standard forms. Examples from the data include:

INF: 'Why [deɪ] you bring me back no shrimps?'
INF: 'I [deɪ] pay nothing.'
INF: 'She [deɪ] even know that she was pregnant.'

3.8.6 The Variable (doPast Neg): Some Data Concerning Usage

At this stage in the discussion of 'do' as operator verb it is appropriate to discuss some data which looks at the forms of both main verb 'do' and operator 'do' in the past tense. The data were collected from all thirty-nine speakers in the sample, and they focus on the variants of the past negative verb form of the verb 'do'. One important methodological decision concerning the investigation of this variable was that of collating operator 'do' with main verb 'do'. Preliminary examination of the data revealed that the same variant forms could appear, regardless of whether 'do' was the operator or the main verb in an utterance. It seems clear that future research could be designed to investigate the incidence of one variant over another dependent on grammatical function; however, the purpose of our analysis was to examine use of variants over time and according to social class, rather than to grammatical function.

The variants of *do*Past Neg, which can appear, are as follows: there is first the ablaut form (discussed in the previous section), which runs [deɪ] throughout the paradigm. There exist then a range of what might be termed intermediate forms. These range from [deɪnt] – a clear mixture of the ablaut vowel, but with a negative particle added – through to [dɪnt], a form which elides only the [d] of the contracted standard form [dɪdnt]. Another intermediary (which preliminary analysis suggests is more commonly found among women) is [diːnt]. It is harder to see where this form fits into any continuum: it has a negative particle attached, suggesting a more standard-like realisation; but conversely, the vowel is a lengthed one, possibly suggesting something closer to the local ablaut form. Finally, there are the standard forms [dɪdnt] and [dɪdnɒt].

Informants had been asked about the ablaut form at interview. Their sheet, 'More about language', had contained three test sentences:

- There was a crash on the M6 last night, but I day see nothing.
- It day seem fair, giving them all that money.
- We day buy it.

It was clear from the data gathered about this that the form is widely known among speakers. Collating results from the test sentences shows that 97.4 per cent of speakers had heard the form in their area, but only 23.15 per cent reported using it. Of the speakers who reported using the form themselves, 66.7 per cent self-declared working-class origin, 55.6 per cent were male, and only the 61–70 age group did not contain any speakers who reported using the form. The most likely age groups to contain speakers reporting using the form were the 27–40 and 41–60 age groups; in each test sentence, three speakers from each of these groups reported using the form.

Qualitative discussion among speakers concerning this variable is well exemplified in the following exchanges:

EA: 'Would either of you use "ay" and "day" and "cor"?'
INF 1: 'No.'

INF 2: 'Erm(.)maybe when I was at school I would have used those more, but I don't(.)I tend not to say them now(.)it's more(.)It's quite conscious that you don't say them I suppose.'
(Asprey 2007: 127)

INF: 'I would never say like "ay" or "day". I would never say that(.)that is something that . . .'
EA: 'Do you hear these things?'
INF: 'Oh all the time(.)that's how everyone speaks(.)everyone around me.'
(Asprey 2007: 128)

EA: 'So "ay"(.)you wouldn't use "ay"(.)does that grate on you as well?'
INF 1: 'It doesn't really grate on me(.)but a lot of people use it.'
INF 2: '"Ay" doesn't(.)"day" does [Laughs](.)"day" is the worst.'
INF 1: 'Yeah, I don't like "day"(.)I don't mind "ay"(.)but . . .'
INF 3: 'A lot of people say "ay".'
EA: 'A lot of people say "ay"(.)and it's also not so far from "ain't".'
INF 2: 'Yeah – I do say "ain't".'
(Asprey 2007: 128)

It is clear that, for these four informants at least, [deɪ] is stigmatised, and they seem more likely to be accepting of local forms for *have*Neg Present and *be*Neg Present. This tallies with evidence presented above which shows a marked difference between use and knowledge of [deɪ].

Quantitative analysis of the variable was difficult, since the forms were recorded at varying levels among informants. Nevertheless, results show that 25.6 per cent of informants actually used the local variant [deɪ] at interview. The figure tallies well with the self-reports the informants gave; usage is very slightly under-reported, but a 2.45 per cent level of difference (in favour of under-reporting) displays remarkable accuracy on the part of those doing the self-reporting.

Of those who reported that they would not use the form, only two informants actually did so at interview. Both were male, and neither displayed animosity towards the variant at interview. One informant used high levels of many local grammatical forms, especially the local forms of *be*Neg Present, *have*Neg Present, and *be*Neg Past. He also used the local system of determiners, and his phonology was very localised. The other, by contrast, did not feel that he spoke a variety which was heavily localised. He talked of having changed the way he spoke when he started work, and it was indeed the case that he did not use many local grammatical forms. His use of the local variant only occurred once (his other two occurrences of the variable were the standard variant).

A breakdown of usage by gender shows three female informants who use the local variant, compared to seven men. There is no age group which did not contain a speaker who uses the local variant, though the age groups containing the least number of informants using the local form are the 27–40 and 61–70 age groups, even though one of the groups most likely to contain speakers reporting that they used the form was the 27–40 age group. There are three informants who reported that they would use the form, but did not in fact do so at interview. The first uses the standard form five times out of five; the second uses it seven times out of seven; and the third uses it once (this is her only use of *do*Neg Past). The second of these three discussed his ideas of situational style shifting, and motivations for it, quite openly at interview, and his comments relate directly to his choosing a fudge form of *have*Neg Present during the interview:

> EA: 'To what extent would you say that you use Black Country grammar(.) You know, to what extent do you say 'I [ei]' and 'I [bei]' and 'I [dei]' and 'I [kɔ:]'(.)Does it depend who you're with?'
> INF: 'Erm, it does a little bit yeah. Because I have to speak to people from other areas of the country on the phone where I work and that, so I but(.) I do use them and things drop in occasionally. Like, you know, I might be [*unclear*] somebody and I'd use the word [mi] instead of [mai](.)I [ei] done [mi] speech [for brother's wedding] yet.'
> EA: 'And you would say [ei]?'
> INF: 'Yeah(.)Or I'd say [eint](.)You've got both(.)Yeah(.)I [eint] done [mi] speech yet(.)I'd probably say "ain't" if I was a little bit unsure(.)It's not I don't even think about it(.)Do you know what I mean?(.)If I was speaking to you I would be more inclined to say "I [eint] done [mi] speech yet" than say "I [ei] done it."'
> EA: 'Why?'
> INF: 'Because(.)I don't, I don't know. Because I don't know you so well(.)And knowing that you're from Walsall(.)I don't really know Esther(.)she's from Walsall(.)She's not necessarily going to understand(.)I'll make myself sound a bit common if I say [ei] and that.'
> (Asprey 2007: 129)

This informant was a speaker Asprey had observed in conversation before as a friend of a friend, and he did, as he reported, use local forms in situations less formal than the interview. However, he used a mixture of the standard, fudge and local forms of *be*Neg Pres and *have*Neg Pres during his interview, and the standard form of *do*Neg Past throughout his interview. He did not restrict himself to only using fudge forms of *have*Neg Pres, as his comments above might suggest; indeed he had already used the local variant [ei] at interview before the exchange given above had taken place. This discrepancy in his own report makes it doubtful he would never use either the local or fudge variants of *do*Neg Past.

In contrast, the other two informants only use the standard variant. The first has five instances of this. There seems no clear motivation for her having reported that she would use the form. She also appears to have over-reported on her interview form her use of the local variant of *have*NEG PRES, since, at interview, she only ever used the standard variant. As an informant she was very enthusiastic, finding many alternatives for each notion word, and was quick to come to the defence of the Black Country area and the language associated with it. Her Identification Questionnaire shows that she identifies positively with the area. It may be that such speakers over-report using variants. Conversely, it may be the case that this speaker chose the use of the standard as her strategy for avoiding the local when interviewed. More research is needed in the Black Country on situational motivation for choosing different variants at different times. The third informant did not discuss his responses to the questions at interview: his was the interview which had to be terminated early due to unacceptable levels of background noise. He only used the variable *do*Neg Past once, and his use of *be*Neg Present shows that he uses both the fudge and standard variants at interview. Had there been more time to collect more instances of *do*Neg Past, other variants might have emerged in his usage. As it is, his low score of the variable amply demonstrates the difficulty of analysing morphological variation in quantitative terms.

All five informants in the sample who used some kind of fudge variant for *do*Neg Past are over the age of fifty. None used the fudge as their only variant of *do*Neg Past. Of the five, two also used the standard form, and three also used the local form. None employed all three strategies. Using the fudge form cannot be convincingly linked to gender; three of those using it were male, and two female. Self-declared class for four out of the five speakers was working class; only one informant declared middle class. It is difficult to see clear lines along which this data can be interpreted since there is not enough data to draw convincing conclusions. Further investigation should focus on the phonological context of each variant, and on devising a methodology which might be more successful at gathering more instances of the variable, which occurs remarkably infrequently in unstructured conversation.

3.8.7 Auxiliary 'have': Affirmative and Negative

The auxiliary 'have' – and indeed the main verb 'have' – have older forms still to be found among much older speakers. Manley gives this paradigm (1971: 45) – shown in Figure 3.15 – together with the verb forms which appear reduced in unstressed position (i.e., when they appear as support before a present or past participle), so that Aux + *give*Past Part appears in the right-hand column of the figure following the verb 'see'. Loss of the second person distinction means that the verb distinction is also lost. Loss of the verbal ending [ən~n] means also that the paradigm is now identical with that of the standard paradigm, and indeed, both operator and main verb 'have' have levelled out at 'have' or 'has'. The negative form is now different. It again employs ablaut and runs as shown on the right of Figure 3.15 (Manley's 1971 older forms being given for comparison on the left).

Finally, the past tense affirmative paradigm of 'have' as both operator and main verb is identical with that of the standard, though past evidence suggests there was once stem levelling to 'has' (Bartlett 1886). We looked at reduced forms of the auxiliary – again the modern local end of the continuum is the same as the West Midlands Standard English end – and gave informants the test sentence 'We'n been playing football.' Of the responses received, 73 per cent of informants had heard the construction. On closer examination at interview, nearly all those who had replied in the affirmative had analysed the construction as '[wiːm] been playing football'. This analysis is incorrect, since the Black Country form [wiːm] is a contraction of the auxiliary 'be' rather than 'have'. It is likely that informants were rationalising an unfamiliar construction.

Present tense affirmative – main verb	Present tense affirmative as auxiliary support
ɒɪ æn	ɒɪn sɪd
ðiː æst	ðɪst sɪd
iː ɜː ɪt æz	ɪz ɜːz ɪts sɪd
wiː æn	wɪn sɪd
jɔʏ æn	jɔʏn sɪd
ðeɪ æn	ðeɪn sɪd

Figure 3.15 Auxiliary Verb 'have': Affirmative Forms (after Manley 1971)

Present tense negative (older)	Present tense negative (newer)
ɒɪ æn → eɪ	ɒɪ æv → eɪ
ði: æst - æsnt	joʊ æv → eɪ
i: ɜ: ɪt æz → eɪ	i: ɜ: ɪt æz → eɪ
wi: æn → eɪ	wi: æv → eɪ
joʊ æn → eɪ	joʊ æv → eɪ
ðeɪ æn → eɪ	ðeɪ æv → eɪ

Figure 3.16 Auxiliary Verb 'have': Negative Forms (after Asprey 2007 and Manley 1971)

3.8.8 Auxiliary 'be': Affirmative and Negative

Even in the sample of present-day Black Country speech there are two competing forms of the main and auxiliary verb 'be'. The normal paradigm in the present tense among speakers closer to the Black Country end of the speech continuum is as follows: two forms of the verb 'be' are given in Figure 3.17 – the positive/negative 'bin'/'bay' combination is the older form, but both the 'bin'/'bay' and the 'am'/'ay' combinations are currently in use in the Black Country. Evidence from Asprey's 2007 data shows this to be so, and Figure 3.17 clarifies it. The forms beginning [b] are, as has been mentioned, dropping rapidly from the speech of all but the most elderly users. The norm at the Black Country end of the continuum is now syncretism with the negative past paradigm of 'have'. In the past form there are also competing variants within the region. In the past, levelling of the verb appears to have taken place in

Present tense negative (older)	Present tense negative (newer)
ɒɪ beɪ	ɒɪ eɪ
ði: bɪsnt	joʊ eɪ
i: ɜ: ɪt æz beɪ	i: ɜ: ɪ eɪ
wi: beɪ	wi: eɪ
joʊ beɪ	joʊ eɪ
ðeɪ βeɪ	ðeɪ eɪ

Figure 3.17 Auxiliary Verb 'be': Negative Forms (after Asprey 2007)

the direction of 'were' forms (as in much of the northern Midlands and the wider north).

Rock (1974:10) makes mention of this, giving the following examples:

'Churchill, when he were exhorting us to fight and carry on . . ."
'When I were young.'

But he concludes that at that time the past tense of the verb to be showed 'a reversal of the pattern in Standard English, for the first person singular is often 'were' . . . and the plural form is often 'was" (1974: 17). In support of this, one of Asprey's informants (2007: 134) says of his aunt's linguistic usage, 'That were her expression anyway', but at other time uses 'was' in the same context. Another informant does the same: 'It was on the right-hand side as you went up over the hill, Danks's were(.)and that's where they used to make all the boilers.' (Asprey 2007: 134).

The overriding tendency now is towards stem levelling at 'was' throughout the paradigm, and only six informants used the 'were' forms at interview, all of them aged over sixty. The usage would seem to have stretched across the Black Country; one informant was born in Wednesbury in the north, and the other in Sedgley, which is to the south.

Examples of informants levelling to 'was' across the data include:

'Where was you born?'
'How old was you then?'
'They was all younger than me.'
'When we was in Nice.'

We can say then that informants vary both past and present tense negation strategies even within a sentence; there is a continuum for them of more and less standard. For present tense 'be' and 'have', such variation is particularly noticeable. An informant produces [tiːnvɛriɒfn] where careful standard speech might have [ɪtɪsnt]. It is clear though that this is a grammatical construction not found in the standard – the fronting of the verb phrase where the standard would be more likely to have the subject pronoun beginning the clause. Her sentence had been '[tiːnvɛriɒfn] you hear that anymore?' This may mean that Black Country local variety speakers have more opportunities to use a reduced form of the verb 'be'. An informant within the same recording dyad mirrors the construction by answering his wife [noʊɪrɪsntnæʊ]. Another repeats the utterance previously given, but this time realises the verb as [tæʔ]. Such reduction lends weight to Britton's theory that some negating strategies are the result of reduced [nt] forms.

3.8.9 Older Strategies for Marking Support and Modality

We suggest that the local Black Country system may have employed a negative marking strategy for verbs which used the suffix [-nə], or at least that a subgroup of Black Country speakers may have done so. Finding rudimentary support from older dialect surveys for this theory is not difficult. Information provided by the informant from Himley in the *SED* suggests that both forms of negative marking have existed within the Black Country. This we find in the *SED*:

> *You might say: Get away, I . . . drunk* and the response given is: [aɪ ɛɪ] or [aɪ ɪnə]
> 'older' [remark made by the informant in explanation]. (Orton and Barry
> 1971: 1,054)

More substantial support is found in the lyrics of songs and in dialect poetry. Bartlett (1886), writing in Bilston, gives many examples:

> S'pose yoh wunna mind a sittin'
> Down a bit on this 'ere bench? . . .

> Bob's bin sent back from the schule,
> And 'ee conna walk – 'ee's lyin'
> On the path be th'owd pit pule . . .

> Un the kids, nor me, nor missus,
> 'ad'na gorra a grub ter eat.

The only auxiliary, modal or 'do' support verb he gives, not formed using this strategy, is the verb 'do', which is negated as 'doh' [doʊ].

Raven and Raven (1966) give the lyrics for *The Battle of Bilston*, a poem without an attested author concerning a cockfight, published in the Bilston Almanac in 1923:

> For he pecked like a miner a-holin',
> And struck clean and straight with his spurs,
> 'By Christ' says Old Bull's Head 'he's a true 'un'
> And let him say he binna, wot dares.

It shows the use of these forms, but also goes on to give the past tense using the [ənt] form 'but the Bils'on cock warn't yet beaten'. It is Raven and Raven (1965: 59–60) who also reproduce the humorous anonymous nineteenth-century poem *Christening the Wench Ben*, set in the Lye (one mile north-east of Stourbridge). In one verse there is both 'dain't you spake?' and 'dunna be taking so silly'. Indeed, examining local variety evidence thoroughly leads to an initial hypothesis that it may have been operator 'do' which was the first verb to conform to the newer negation strategies of first -nt marking, and later, vowel mutation. 'Have' and 'be' appear to remain negated using the [-nə] strategy for longer, as do the modal verbs.

Evidence from dialect poetry suggests that different strategies of negative verb marking have been in competition over the past two centuries (and maybe earlier, though any evidence of this is still to be found). A more standard strategy [nt], a Midlands strategy of [nə], and an emergent strategy employing ablaut rather than suffixation have all existed. Freeman (1930) is of the opinion that:

> A hundred years ago two forms of dialect were in common use in the Black Country. Naturally they were closely akin and had many terms in common, but the accent with which they were spoken was noticeably different; the one native to the immediate district was direct and emphatic, while the other, brought by the mining families from the neighbouring County of Shropshire, was softer and intoned with a musical lilt.

This popular idea was articulated by many of the informants as well, though some replaced the influence of the intonation of Shropshire with that of Welsh incomers. On the basis of his theory, Freeman concludes that a gulf between 'native dialect' and 'Shropshire dialect' was the reason for the /nə/ forms which appeared, as opposed to 'native' forms such as 'I who', 'I cor', 'I doh' (his respelling). We suggest instead that the oldest strategy /nə/, though possibly reinforced by incomers from Shropshire, was the original native form. We hypothesise that a standard strategy of [nt] came in to the area, allowing forms like 'dain't' [deint], 'ain't' [eint], 'int' [ɪnt], and that these forms were reduced, their vowels nasalised, and eventually, that the suffix was lost to produce total reliance on vowel mutation to mark time difference. Intermediate morphological forms also exist, and the semantic changes they have undergone can be documented using historical evidence. Manley (1971: 57) reports that the 'addition' of [t] to negative verb forms marks emphasis:

> When the negative forms /dei, ei, bei, ʃɔː, wɔː, ɛː, kɔː/ occur finally in the sentence, 't' is added to them; this usually, though not always, indicates some degree of emphasis on the part of the speakers (contempt, disgust, etc.):

e.g.   /dɪstlaɪkɜː/?   /ɒdeɪt/!
        /kɒstdiʊɛtnaʊ/?   /ɒkɔːt/!

Britton (1992: 48) does not believe that the Black Country forms derive from [-nə] forms:

> Could it be that all the enclitic-deleted forms are actually derived from /nə/ negatives and not from /nt/ forms at all? The answer ... is an appropriately negative one: the evidence for diachronic and synchronic variation between forms with /t/ and Ø argues powerfully against derivation of the Ø forms from /nə/ forms, as also does the difficulty of deriving [deː] from [dɪdnt] ... [doʊ] transparently derives from [doʊ(n)t] rather than [dʊnə]; and ... [eː] cannot descend from [anə] or [ɪnə] but must have its ultimate origin in [eːnt].

3.8.10 Modal Verbs: Affirmative and Negative

Certain modal verbs still use the strategy of ablaut. Figure 3.18 (from Manley 1971: 41–6) gives the paradigms for the verbs 'can', 'shall' and 'will' in the second person singular affirmative and negative forms.

Of those given, 'will' and 'can' still have relatively high levels of use among all ages at the Black Country end of the speech continuum. We asked informants about *can*Neg Present in a questionnaire, and found that 92 per cent hear the construction, with 36 per cent reporting that they used it. Of those who used it, 42 per cent were under forty. What does seem likely is that younger speakers are bringing the form closer to the standard [kɑːnt] by using [kɑː], which derives from the standard [kan] rather than Black Country local variety [kɒn]. So one finds, for example: 'Erm, I [kɑː] think of any others' (Asprey 2007: 138).

We had asked informants about [kɑː] in the sentence 'You can paint the fence again if you like, but I cor see the point myself.' Bizarrely, one informant reported using the variant when she had not reported hearing it. It transpired, however, that she now lives in Wombourne, having been born in Stourbridge, and does not report the variant for Wombourne, but uses it herself.

joʊ kan ~ kɒn	a ~ ɒ → ɔː	joʊ kɔː
joʊ ʃal	a → ɛː	joʊ ʃɛː
joʊ wɪl	ɪ → oʊ	joʊ woʊ

Figure 3.18 Affirmative and Negative Verb Forms (after Manley 1971)

3.8.11 Auxiliary Support for Modal Verbs

The usual support verb at the local end of the speech continuum for the modal verbs 'ought' and 'should' is 'have'. Constructions such as 'I hadn't ought to have gone' are common at the more local end of the variety continuum, even among younger speakers. Higgs reports using this and being unaware of its variation from the standard until he left the area (2004: 60). It does appear to be below the level of consciousness, but was never remarked on at interview, even during highly detailed discussions about Black Country grammar with informants, and is not infrequently used: 'We ought to have Ron here(.)hadn't we?' (Asprey 2007: 139).

'Used to'

Related to the construction of tag questions with certain modal verbs is the construction of auxiliary support with the compound verb 'used to'. In the same way as the modals previously discussed take 'have' as support, so this construction also takes 'have' as support and interrogative tag. Thus one informant remarks 'They'd used to call we Brummies(.)hadn't they?' (Asprey 2007: 139).

3.8.12 Conditional Constructions

There are a few constructions peculiar to the area to which Higgs (2004: 56) calls his readers' attention. He examines what he calls past 'have' in conditional sentences, and shows that the structure is 'HAVE (past) + HAVE (infinitive) + ED'. He gives 'I wished I hadn't have had them' as an example of this.

3.9 More about Aspect and Mood

In common with other varieties which border the Black Country in regional terms, especially to the north of the region, Black Country grammar has a construction which is used in the subjunctive mood, described by Biber et al. (2002: 60) as 'the form of a finite verb that is sometimes used in hypothetical or non-factual cases'. In one main verb 'wish', speakers, especially those in middle age or later, make use of 'wished' rather than West Midlands Standard English 'wish'. Thus, utterances such as 'I wished I lived in a big house like that', or 'I wished I were a postman', are used not to mark past time events; rather they mark irrealis. Whether or not this marks a use of the subjunctive on a broader scale than is found in Standard English, it is certainly a construction very commonly used in the area. An informant remarked at interview:

> 'And I used to say to him, I said dad, I wished you wouldn't use so much bone dust(.)I said it's bound to make you ill.' (Asprey 2007: 139)

Asprey (2007: 140) documents the existence marker [ə] (orthographically [a]) to indicate continuous action, which can be found among older speakers in the Black Country. Thorne (2003: 71) also makes reference to this in a BhamEng context. Asprey reports on Higgs (2004: 62), working in the south-western Black Country. The progressive negative aspect is something Higgs discusses before: he found evidence in his sample of a-prefixing on the lexical verb following auxiliary support in both past and present time. This prefixing is explained by Wakelin (1972: 120) as deriving from the Old English ōn prefix which was used for the verbal noun, but which is now used not for the noun, but for the verb in the Black Country. Wolfram's (1991b) descriptive account of a-prefixing in Virginia USA, shows that the phenomenon is under similar prosodic, phonetic and syntactic constraints there as it is in the Black Country. Thus, in the Black Country as in Virginia, forms like 'he likes the a-fishing on that bit of the canal' are not possible. On the other hand, 'He was out a-fishing yesterday', is possible. Wolfram (1991b: 233) remarks that 'A-sailin' is fun' is ungrammatical, and that the syntactic constraint depends on the fact that the form does 'appear to fit the classical definition of a gerund construction'. Similarly, a-prefixing in the Black Country, as in Virginia, does not occur on adjectival forms (Wolfram gives 'the hunters saw the a-runnin' bear'). Finally, there is no possibility of the a-prefix being realised unless 'the initial syllable of a verb base is stressed'. He gives sentences like 'He was a-manipulatin' things to demonstrate this.

The construction is found in the south of the Black Country in Asprey's data, and only in the speech of the oldest informants. One informant gives utterances such as: 'I've just been [aseijin] you know(.) when I told you I was [əpʊɾin] little things down' (Asprey 2007: 140).

Another, asked about words which mean fighting, gives 'fisticuffs [ɐfɑɪtɪn]'. While it is apparent that the construction was once the norm (dialect folk songs and poetry tell us this), it is now restricted to older speakers in the Black Country.

Thorne (2003: 71) reports that:

> The letter 'a', having phonological variants ranging from [a] to [ə], is regularly added as a prefix in the speech of older working-class Brummies to the

present participle of verbs such as 'come', 'go', 'walk', 'play', 'stand', 'tell' and 'knock' when in the past or present continuous tenses, e.g, 'You en't a-tellin' me what to have!' ... 'The two girls was a-playin' out' ... 'I still used to go a-socialising down Hockley.'

In the same way, Tennant (1982: 19) gives the example 'oimagunna' for what he glosses as 'I am going to', and (1982: 25) 'wuzzagunna' for 'I did intend to' or 'I was intending to'. He gives the example 'Oi wuzzagunna gew today but oi intagunna gew till tomorra — then oi amagunna gew fuddeffinit' (1982: 26). It seems likely from the evidence given that this feature is recessive within the city of Birmingham, and indeed, in the neighbouring Black Country.

There is one instance which parallels the *SED* construction of [ə] + past participle, which occurs with an informant when she is asked for her word for 'television': 'It was [əkɔːɫd gɒgbɒks] when we'd had it first' (Asprey 2007: 140). The example is most clear and not open to interpretation on the part of the transcriber; it is clear, however, that one instance of a construction could just be an anomaly. Trudgill (1999: 87) also notes the 'way in which Standard English speakers say things like *I don't want any trouble* with only one negative ... while speakers of most other dialects use older forms such as *I don't want no trouble* with more than one negative.' In this, the local Black Country variety follows the pattern of most regional varieties. Speakers say 'I ay got none', 'I day see nothing', combining the unusual negated verb forms peculiar to the variety with another negative. Manley (1971: 58) gives the construction:

[ɑː deɪ	av	neːɹən]
I do OperatorPast Neg	have Past Part	Adv any Neg
(Literally: 'never a one')		

which an elderly female informant gave a standard gloss of 'I didn't have one.' An informant in Asprey's 2007 data gives 'I ain't never thought about that one.' In the *SED*, triple negatives are found at Himley in the live recording made in 1955 by Ellis (see Orton and Barry 1969: 7); thus an informants remarks that 'he hadn't got no twig off no tree'. Since double negatives are stigmatised throughout the English-speaking world, in the Black Country they inspire comments such as:

I hate it when I hear myself say it(.)like(.)'I didn't do nothing'(.)double negatives(.)I think it makes us sound stupid(.)which is probably why people from other parts of the country think so.(Asprey, 2007: 141)

It is clear that investigating the incidence of double negatives in the Black Country would yield results. Indeed, the sentence 'There was a crash on the M6 last night, but I day see nothing.' was given to informants, and answers revealed that speakers reported hearing double negatives at 92.3 per cent. Only three speakers said that they did not hear the variant in their areas, and one of these was from the overspill village for Wolverhampton, Perton (built in the early 1980s). She reported at interview that, having lived in Bilston most of her life, she found Perton 'posh', and she herself used double negatives at interview. However, only 23 per cent of informants reported using the construction. In retrospect, this may again be something to do with the influence of the extreme local form [deɪ], which was used in the sentence to lend authenticity. If double negatives are as underused as the results might suggest, this may be a direct result of Asprey having put two non-standard features in the text, the second of which may be more heavily stigmatised. Perhaps a sentence like 'He didn't see nobody.' would have elicited different results, though examples were found across the span of data:

> INF: 'I [deɪnt?] do nothing.'
> INF: 'Why [deɪ] you bring me back no shrimps?'

Discourse Particle 'like'

In recent years, sociolinguists have reported on the rise of the discourse particle 'like', both as a quotative mechanism and as a filler (see Macaulay 2001; Tagliamonte and D'Arcy 2004). Older Black Country residents vary in the way they employ the particle 'like' as a filler to focus on certain aspects of a clause. Younger residents follow the pattern highlighted by Macaulay; that is, they place 'like' before the main information. Some speakers, however, place focusing 'like' after the crucial information. It might appear that the phenomenon is restricted to older speakers, since one might be tempted to conclude that the two strategies could not coexist. In this way, people in the 71+ age group give utterances such as 'And they've got in there a word "puck up"(.)instead of "pick up"(.)like'. One finds, however, that this is by no means the case. The phenomenon carries through to the younger generations, even though they exist within a linguistic community their own age which uses 'like' in utterance medial position:

> INF: 'To work there you've got to be able to take a laugh(.)and a joke like.'
> INF: 'Cause they could say some stuff that could hurt you like.'
> INF: 'And then go out and do it on our own like.'
> (Asprey 2007: 142)

The two functions seem closely related. And though some have argued that they have become almost empty categories, we would argue that they fulfil a focusing role in both cases; mid-utterance, they serve as a pause before new information, and utterance finally they serve as a focuser to refer the listener back to the important information which went before.

Quotative 'be like' and Quotative 'go'

In both Glasgow (Macaulay) and Toronto (Tagliamonte and D'Arcy) it is reported that young people used 'like' between two clauses as a mechanism for indicating the appearance of reported speech in the second clause, most usually as a replacement for the verb 'say': 'She's sitting there and she's like, "Oh my god!" She's like, "That's your boyfriend". And I'm like "Yeah"' (Tagliamonte and D'Arcy 2004: 493).

This phenomenon is found in the construction both of quotative 'like' and of filler 'like'. Macaulay (2001: 17) gives a clearer example of focus 'like'. By this, we can understand a use of the particle to provide emphasis – a pause before important information is revealed towards the end of an utterance: 'He'll stop breathing, and you'll go like, 'Oh my God – he's like suffocating.'

Both younger and older Black Country residents display a tendency to use quotative 'like' between two clauses (this makes sense since quotative 'like' has the function of introducing reported speech and must appear before the speech it reports). When given the test sentence, 'He was like, "It's daft being afraid of the dark".', only 36 per cent of informants reported actually hearing the construction, and only 13 per cent reported using it themselves. It may be that the form 'go' is still in competition with the newer strategy, and certainly 'say' in 'narrative tense' ('Anyway, he thought I'd better go back to the doctor's, so I says to him, "I shall have to, I suppose".', was the test sentence informants were given) is much in evidence, even among young people. We hear from young informants utterances like:

> INF: 'That's what Dil in the shop says(.)he says(.)always ask the [mɪsɪz] for ten Embassy [dʊndɑːːz] [cigarettes] cause she's proper Indian.'
> INF: 'Mum was like "oh no".'
> INF: 'My grandad was like an ambassador.'
> INF: 'I goes [gəz] well [doʊ] his family mind?'
> (Asprey 2007: 143)

Twenty-six per cent of informants had never heard of 'narrative tense' 'say'. On the other hand, 72 per cent did use it. It is possible that 'say' competes with 'be like' and is still more widely used. Certainly eight out of the eleven informants who reported using 'like' were under twenty-seven.

Buchstaller (2004) used matched guise tests to investigate social perceptions of quotative 'like' use (together with that of quotative 'go') in the UK. She asked informants to read a transcript which contained instances of quotative 'like', and to judge the class, gender and age of the speaker (in fact a seventeen year-old working-class woman). She found that UK judges of who used 'be like' were undecided about whether it was a working-class or middle-class variant, or male or female variant. However, 85 out of 101 informants did agree that the speaker was likely to be thirty or younger (2006: 369). As a variant spreading into the Black Country, community recognition and evaluation of it might tell us more about the linguistic models which speakers are choosing – if levels of its use are higher among younger people – and it is a possible way of signalling youth identity within the Black Country.

3.10 Conclusion

A thorough analysis of several distinctive features of the local Black Country variety has shown that it is not the pure Anglo-Saxon the BBC Voices correspondents at the start of the chapter thought. There has always been variation and change within the dialect, and there is strong evidence that in the most distinctive part of the morphological system, the support verb subsystem, the strategy of ablaut negation has developed relatively recently. Britton's 1992 discussion of the Black Country variety and its verbal negation strategies suggests that the majority of those forms are based unequivocally on reductions of the standard colloquial forms ending in [nt], rather than on the older negation strategy of [nə]. There is strong backing for his theory in the similarity between the vowel quality of the standard colloquial negated verb forms, and the vowel remaining after the negative particle [nt] is lost. In other words, the Black Country, far from containing historically unchanged morphological features, seems in this instance to have been subject to a standardising influence. It is possible that such an influence could be traced by examining migration patterns within the area; certainly, the abundance of work in the new industries of mining and metalwork (which became available from the eighteenth century onwards) was a factor in bringing incomers to the area. There is much historical and present-day literature on census data which has already helped to clarify such patterns of in-migration, and a careful examination of the historical linguistic evidence, backed with literature concerning population movement, might provide a more definite answer concerning the rise of this unusual negation strategy.

Certainly the most remarkable thing about the way the Black Country speech community itself perceives the variety is their insistence on its historical pedigree. This study strongly suggests, in view of the evidence presented that, in one respect at least, the variety is far more affected by the standardisation process than are the traditional varieties in neighbouring areas. It shares these newer forms of verbal negation with the neighbouring city of Birmingham, and could be said to be a traditional local variety which has been subject to levelling over the past 100 years; certainly Ellis (1889: 463) reported these new forms, remarking that 'it [the transcription] gives a good conception of the Black Country speech. The peculiar form of the negative is well brought out.'

In a similar way, the grammar of the Black Country local variety contains much which is also found across the UK in other dialects. It shares with other varieties the strategy of zero plural marking, and the relative pronouns 'what' and 'as' for standard 'that'. Hughes and Trudgill (1996: 20) remark that unmarked plurality is 'a very widespread feature indeed', and that in terms of relative pronouns, 'the form with *what* is particularly common' (1996: 18). Many forms which can be proven (through historical evidence from Ellis (1889) and the *SED*) to be more localised, are being lost. Thus, zero plural marking following proximal determiners – like the example 'these cabbitch' cited from Rock (1974: 14) – is not found in the data. Though this by no means assures us that the structure is extinct, it strongly suggests that such forms are now much rarer. In contrast, the supralocal non-standard strategy of zero plural marking following numerals is common in the data.

Related to this is the retention of other features, such as the lack of contrast between adverbial and adjectival forms, which Hughes and Trudgill (1996: 20) claim is typical of 'most non-standard dialects of English', while distinctions such as the older contrast between singular and plural second person pronoun forms in 'thee' and 'thou' are almost entirely lost ([ði] is found only once in the whole data set). In this instance, the distinction was once widespread across the English-speaking world, and persists more strongly in certain areas of the UK. The feature is a distinctive one, however, and what is suggested in this conclusion is that both some locally *and* some supralocally distinctive features are being lost in the Black Country, so that the distinctiveness which persists is comprised of structures not peculiar to the Black Country alone, as well as being a diluted distinctiveness in comparison with the local variety of a hundred years ago. Though one could by no means claim that in-migration into the area has been at such levels as to constitute a 'melting-pot' situation, dialect contact would seem to have caused dialect levelling. The examples given in this paragraph are evidence in favour of the third principle of dialect contact outlined by Kerswill and Williams (1994: 7) that 'marked regional forms are disfavoured . . . forms which have a restricted regional currency, or which are stereotyped as such, generally do not appear in the new variety'.

The preceding paragraphs have presented evidence about the structure of the Black Country variety which indicates that the tendency towards the levelling out and abandoning of distinctive local and supralocal forms over time is clear. On the other hand, it is clear that certain regionally marked forms can take the place of those lost in marking out local distinctiveness. So, although some of the distinctive ablaut negation in the Black Country has disappeared (the negative form of 'shall' as [ʃɛ:], for example, is rarely heard today), many ablaut forms are in common use, even among the young.

Further evidence for the retention of regional forms in the west Midlands is the extent to which the western Midlands third person female subject pronoun form [ɜ:(ɹ)] is used. Again, this distinctive form is used widely, even among the youngest members of the speech community, despite being stigmatised within the community. It is too simplistic to say that the Black Country variety is losing all regional and localised distinctiveness, and too sweeping a generalisation to say that the contributors to the BBC Voices site were wrong to claim the Black Country as one of the oldest and 'purest' varieties in the UK. The truth lies somewhere in between; among the oldest members of the speech community, many grammatical forms with a proven western Midlands pedigree are still in use, and even among the young, western Midlands forms, such as third person [ɜ:], are in common use. Even disputing that *all* the distinctive forms in the Black Country have a long-term historical provenance, it is still clear that the Black Country speech community does preserve a system of negation which is extremely distinctive, not being found anywhere else in the UK, except to a limited extent in neighbouring Birmingham.

Though no attempt has been made in this chapter at a formal analysis and stratification of grammatical variants by age, gender or social class, we can still see that there is change over time in the grammatical structure of the variety, and an analysis of gender and class as extralinguistic factors related to this change would be an obvious focus for future analysis. The final pattern to come out of the data presented here relates, again, to change across time, but is rather more suggestive of one group leading the change, since previous research exists to back this assertion. The rise of quotative 'like', where the older strategy in the Black Country appears to have been quotative 'go', is evidence of the rise of a phenomenon documented in the USA and Canada before it was documented in the UK (see Buchstaller 2004; Macaulay 2001; Tagliamonte and D'Arcy 2004). Preliminary evidence suggests that quotative 'like' is found at higher levels among the young, though there does not appear to be significant gender stratification.

On a related note, the difference between focuser 'like' appearing at the end or start of a stretch of information is evidence of more complex change over time. It is by no means certain what has prompted the shift from final to initial position for this particle, and it is not always the case that speakers of any age group use one strategy exclusively; rather, all age groups use a mix of both.

In conclusion, it can be said that Birmingham and Black Country grammar is subject to levelling in response to supralocal influences (though this levelling is not always prompted by use of the standard – for example, it would be very difficult to argue that use of relative 'what' is in any way standard). It can also be seen, however, that though some local structures are now the preserve of the elderly, others, clearly marked as local, are widely used cross-generationally. It is also the case that change over time has always happened, and though there are residents who claim that Black Country grammar has changed very little, there is significant evidence that this is untrue. Change over time continues to happen, though stable norms are slow to appear following a period of change, as witnessed by the shift from information final 'like' to information initial 'like'. Birmingham and Black Country grammar is by no means immune to contact with other varieties; it does, however preserve some very distinctive local structures across the generations.

4 Lexis

4.1 Introduction

In this chapter, we give examples of words which may be perceived to be declining in terms of attrition and loss of lexical variation, and the restriction of lexical items to specific contexts. We also, to some extent, debunk the myth that lexical variation is declining on an unprecedented scale. Instead, we point to lexical revitalisation, despite the fact that words which are no longer in use due to changes in working practices are in use by even the youngest working generation. For example, although there has been attrition and loss in the words related to highly specific cottage industries such as nail- and chain-making in the Black Country and glass-blowing in Birmingham, lexical phrases such as 'all around the Wrekin' for talking in a circumlatory way, or 'bostin' to denote 'very good', are still very much in use. It is our contention that, rather than lexis being as closely associated with regionally based working practices as it once was, certain words and phrases continue to be used, and enregistered as emblematic of the region, as Chapter 1 has discussed. This is particularly the case in performance events, where regional variants of words and phrases are used as emblematic of, and markers of, a specific regional variety, used in a self-reflexive way.

It is also our contention that communities and boundaries can be self-defining rather than being delineated by geography: it is then extremely difficult to define the speech community being investigated, even if an investigator is a native of the geographical area to be studied. The similarities and differences that define and delimit communities linked to geographical place and space are often not a matter for objective assessment, but are largely subjective, existing as much in the minds of members of the community as with a specific regionally defined place. The Black Country region in particular, as discussed in Chapter 1, is an excellent example of this problematic definition of a speech community and a region.

4.2 The Survey of Regional English (SuRE) and Sense Relations Networks (SRNs)

The most important point to make regarding the SuRE methodology (as outlined in Chapter 1) is that because it asks for 'words you would hear in your local area', it is very difficult to determine which words inform-ants actually use on a day-to-day basis without close questioning. The surest analysis we can conduct is to see if notions pattern regionally, or for age, gender and self-declared social class; then to inform this analy-sis with comments made by informants at interview. Consequently, notions are examined in terms of variation by age, region, gender and social class. Those which are reported by informants as Black Country specific are examined, as are lexical attrition and, conversely, lexical growth in the form of neologism, contact and possible semantic shift. Seven notions are discussed in close detail here, all of which have been selected because they exhibit either considerable variation or very little variation:

Number	Notion word
1	Hit
2	Play truant
3	Tell tales on someone
4	Left-handed
5	Sweets
6	Running water smaller than a river
7	Dog

Figure 4.1 Chosen Lexical Notions for Examination (Asprey 2007: 157)

Analysis here follows the framework devised by Macafee (1994, 2003) and her large-scale investigation of Glaswegian lexical usage to shed light on issues of growth, shift and attrition. This introduces differ-ent strands of investigation. The first is the continuum between older informants' active use of certain items, through receptive use, to loss among the youngest age groups. At the same time, lexical usage among the young raises questions about the provenance of newer items. Macafee (1994: 70–1) outlines three stages of lexical erosion, the first point of which being the shift from active to passive knowledge, and the second being the erratic survival of words in the speech community, in that they can become idiolectal, rather than dialectal – i.e. the property of particular speakers. Thirdly, a linked point is the shift from unrestricted everyday use to occasional use, more or less within quotation marks. Words thus become fossilised in particular registers. According to Macafee, songs and rhymes are important categories in this respect, and can probably preserve passive vocabulary indefinitely. Data from the West Midlands Dialect Project (WMDP) project however, discussed below, suggests that rather than becoming fossilised, certain words and phrases become enregistered as emblematic of a specific dialect.

Finally, the decision to investigate certain notions as being Black Country specific was taken by examining comments made by informants, as well as matching those comments to a small corpus of dictionaries of Black Country dialect across time. The corpus is a diachronic one, comprising five dictionaries, one glossary, and two newspaper articles, which asked readers of the paper to nominate their favourite Black Country dialect words.

4.2.1 'Hit'

There are thirteen different responses for the notion 'hit' given on the written forms which informants complete before they are interviewed. The notion is a particularly productive one: seven informants give more than one response, and three informants give four or more responses. The alternative, which is of particular interest here, is 'lamp'. It is given by six informants as their primary alternative for 'hit' (i.e. the first alternative written down on their sheet), and by five informants as their secondary alternative, making it the most frequently given alternative. It is a good example of an alternative which is not stratifiable by gender. Six women report it, and five men. It is not stratifiable by region of the Black Country – informants using it come from as far north as Wolverhampton and Wednesfield, centrally in Dudley, and as far south as Pensnett. Of those who give it, four are in the 27–40 age group, four in the 41–60 age group, two in the 61–70 age group, and one in the 71 + age group. The only group who do not report hearing the word are the 16–26 age group. An example from the data is: 'They used to use that give him a lamping(.)but I mean I haven't heard that for years(.)mind you I'm just trying to think did we hear that in the town not so long ago a woman had got a small child [ə] says if you don't stop it I'll give you a lamping.' This suggests that usage is high among those in the middle age ranges, but declines with age. However, this does not tie in well with the corpus evidence that can be cited. As early as 1930, Freeman

Date	Author	Medium	Source
1930	Shaw	Book	A glossary of Black Country words and phrases
1930	Freeman	Glossary	Black Country stories and sketches
1974	Wilson	Book	Staffordshire dialect words: a historical survey
1979	Raven	Book	Aynuk's second Black Country waerd buk
1998	Beach	Online book	'Ow we spake' – The dialect of the Black Country
undated (1990s)	Walker	Book	The definitive Black Country dictionary
2004	Chinn (ed)	Newspaper article	'Recalling our sayings from days of the past'
2005	Ogden (ed)	Newspaper article	'Sharrap – it's our lingo!'

Figure 4.2 Structure of the Corpus of Black Country English

in his glossary gives 'lamping' for a thrashing, and in support of its being a long-standing variant, Wilson (1974) in his *Staffordshire Dialect Words* gives 'lamp' as 'beat', 'thrash'. Five out of six informants who give the alternative as their primary choice are self-declared as working class, and only one middle-class speaker did so.

It becomes clear that the alternative 'lamp' itself is commented on by many at interview, and that in semantic terms there is a good level of agreement among informants about it, and its range of meanings. It can be said with certainty then that informants across the age groups who use the alternative agree that, while it does mean 'hit', it is most usually to be collocated with the disciplining of children. This is a good example of cohesion and agreement among a speech community. It is used by both men and women, and while it is not used by the youngest informants, this may be due to the changes speakers make throughout their life stages. Certainly none of the informants under twenty-six had children, which might mean that their need for this alternative does not yet exist. It is now illegal to smack children, which means also that the alternative might plausibly undergo attrition in the future. The most important points to make concern the semantic stability of the item, and its frequency as an alternative among the working class.

4.2.2 Play Truant

From the data, the alternative most widely used is 'skive'. The next most cited first alternative is 'wag' or 'wag it', or 'hop the wag'. Of all alternatives, only 'skive' is listed in the dialect corpus, by Walker (undated: 32), and he lists it with the meaning 'stay away from work'. The important qualitative evidence informing analysis at this point is that given by those over sixty. They stress how difficult and risky it was to stay away from school. Parental control was tight, and the 'school mon' or 'school board man' would visit the houses of children reported absent from school to check that their absence was genuine. For example, one informant stresses that 'Everybody used to be frightened to death of stopping away.' It is perhaps because of this that the alternatives listed for those over seventy only include two instances in seven primary alternatives of 'skive'. Informants in this age group often struggle to produce a phrase, and are forced to compromise with alternatives such as 'don't go', 'day off', and 'have one off'. Unravelling this notion and its alternatives, then, is complex.

If we turn now to the examination of the alternative 'wag' and 'wag it'. These are reported as first alternative by two informants in the 16–26 age group, by one in the 27–40 age group, by three in the 41–60 age group, and not by informants above this age. Examining second responses as well as first responses, we find that a further one informant in the 27–40 age group reports the word, a further two informants in the 41–60 age group, and one informant in the 71+ age group. In terms of age patterning, 'wag' and its variants seem to be in use predominantly among those aged 41–60. This is not to say that it has not been heard of or reported among younger informants. Here again the ironic compromise which the SuRE methodology contains is apparent, for its open instructions about 'words you think are local to the area you live in', followed by 'words that you use every day when talking to friends' means in practice that some informants settle for reporting what they consider to be very local words, even if they do not use them themselves, and some report only the words they used. Short of extremely lengthy interviews, it is hard to know how information concerning genuine everyday use of an alternative could be reliably elicited. Instead, we rely here again on qualitative comments made by some informants at interview. Thus an informant in the 27–40 age group reported that she uses nothing but 'wag' in Darlaston (to the north of the fieldwork area):

INF: 'At school it was always wagging(.)we never used anything else except wagging.'
INT: 'Yeah, that's what your mum said too(.)but the van that drives round Walsall . . .'
INF: 'The waggy man! The [wagin] wagon!! [Laughs]

It is clear that, in the school attended by this informant, the alternative was very widely used, particularly since she reports the extension of the verb to the adjective describing both educational welfare officers and their vans. It is possible that this word exhibits interschool variation within one age group. On the other hand, other informants (one schooled in Stourbridge – though not the same school – and the other in Wolverhampton) reported that they always used 'skive' and never 'wag', though it is in their receptive vocabulary. They reported that no one in their schools had used it. In age terms then, it appears that regional patterning cannot explain why some young people who attended a particular school did not use 'wag' while others did. An informant aged twenty-eight at the time of interview, who had reported using 'skive', said: 'Skiving, skiving or wagging, but more so skiving – wagging is one that I've heard(.)but I would say if you weren't going to school you were skiving(.)that's an old word wag it.'

This, in the face of evidence which suggests that the word was indeed in use among her peers, suggests that there is indeed variation between schools concerning the alternatives used. In gender terms, if we collate primary and secondary reports of 'wag' as an alternative, there is an equal split of five reports each between the genders; though for a primary alternative, five women report 'wag' and variants, while only two men do so. In social-class terms, however, there is a clear correlation between positive reporting of the alternative 'wag' and self-declared working-class origin. Five of the six informants reporting 'wag' and variants of it are working class, and only one is middle class. Like the notion 'hit', alternatives which diverge from more standard colloquial alternatives are more commonly used by working-class speakers.

Turning now to the alternative 'skive', Walker's definition of the alternative as not attending work, rather than school, was also articulated by several informants at interview. An informant who reported 'bunk off' as his primary alternative, and who was sixty-four at the time of recording, remarked:

> INF: 'Erm, skive was not confined to school(.)and at work(.)skiver(.)skiving would be skiving off work yes(.)or at work skiving *at* work.'
> INT: 'So going off for a fifteen-minute break when you should have been doing more.'
> INF: 'Yeah(.)yeah.'

There is, however, a conflicting report from one partner in the dyad, aged nineteen at the time of recording, who said that: 'Well, I would wag work, but if I was at school I'd probably be like oh I'm skiving.'

Another partner in the dyad, who was also nineteen, did not agree with him and felt that 'wag' related directly to school, and 'skive' to work. It may be that as it becomes more possible to miss school, the alternative for missing work is being transferred to the school environment, and is recognised by those who use it as being still acceptable for the act of missing work. Perhaps it is important to some speakers to preserve a distinction between the two environments by choosing different alternatives depending on the environment. It is a fact, however, apart from one instance, that no other user of the alternative 'wag' reports that one can 'wag' work.

There may then be a correlation between 'wag' and gender since more women than men chose it as their primary alternative. There is a direct correlation between age and the use of any kind of non-standard term for 'playing truant', in that those brought up in the time when missing school was not possible struggle to find any alternative. Finally, there is a connection between the use of 'skive' for missing work and its rising use among younger speakers for playing truant, which suggests that it is now acceptable for use in the school environment as well as the workplace. It is possible that 'skive' may replace 'wag' as a widely used alternative, a theory evidenced by the lower levels of reporting 'wag' as the primary alternative among 16–26 year-olds.

The final alternative we look at here is 'trotter'. The informant who gave 'trotter' as his primary alternative considers that 'wag' was 'more a West Brom [Bromwich] thing' and reported that 'that wasn't a word we used(.)"skiving"'. He was born in West Bromwich and moved away in early childhood (though precisely when is uncertain). He now lives in Bilston. Another informant who also gave 'trotter' came from from Tipton, some two miles away. It is possible that the alternative is a localised one, though hard to say categorically in the face of a lack of evidence.

4.2.3 Tell Tales on Someone

The alternative most frequently given is 'grass'. Alternatives relating to the act of telling tales which fall very close to the standard, or indeed are the standard, could reasonably be collated and would then form the second most common primary alternative, with ten informants giving the standard 'tell tales on someone' and five informants giving an alternative containing the lexeme 'tell'.

The sample, split by age group, shows that the two alternatives most affected by age variation are 'grass' and 'tell tales'/'tell on'/'telling'/'telling stories'. Levels of use of the alternative 'grass' are 62.5 per cent among the 16–26 age group, falling in the 27–40 age group, and rising to their highest level of 85 per cent among the 41–60 age group; but they are at zero for both age groups over 60. Conversely, more standard alternatives such as 'telling tales', 'telltale' and 'telltale twit' are lowest, at 12.5 per cent, in the youngest age group, rise to 37.5 per cent among the 27–40 age group, yet fall to zero among the 41–60 age group. Levels pick up again to 62.5 per cent in the 61–70 age group, but fall to 14.3 per cent among the 71+ age group.

These patterns are complex, but there is one which can be picked out. It is true that if an informant is under sixty, they are more likely to use the alternative 'grass'; and conversely, if they are over sixty, they are more likely to use an alternative containing the morpheme 'tell'. It is also true that the group with the most variation in terms of alternatives chosen is the 71+ age group. Informants in this age group gave six different primary alternatives. Therefore, it certainly appears that 'grass' is now associated with speakers under sixty. The real issue when analysing lexis becomes pertinent here; it is summarised succinctly by the informant who talks about language change through her lifetime, and says of the alternatives she has marked as her primary choices: 'You latch on to them because like you're hearing them all the time and you forget about what's been said in the past.'

She has made a crucial point: that is that attrition of a particular alternative cannot be proven by looking at change in apparent time. The notion of telling tales on someone, linked with childhood as it is, might well be imagined to be less needed as one goes through life, and one could reasonably suggest that alternatives associated strongly with school might be dropped in favour of alternatives which have semantic associations with adult usage. In support of this theory, Asprey (2001) found that possible neologisms such as 'twag' for 'to tell tales' were in use in the Black Country. 'Twag' is not an alternative given by any informant in this present study on their written forms, yet pilot work had shown that the word does exist in the area, and informants were therefore asked about it during this study at interview. They reported unanimously that it is a word restricted to the school context, and many younger informants remembered it when prompted at interview. One informant recalls: 'I haven't heard "twag". I used to hear that at primary school, so we're talking like early eighties.' And another said: '"Twagging"(.)That I vaguely remember from [mi] childhood(.) playgroundy.'

4.2.4 Left-handed

Sixty-seven per cent of informants gave the alternative 'caggy-handed' [kagi(h)andid] for this notion. In addition, 5 per cent gave 'cacky-handed'. Adding these two informants in with their related forms to these figures means that 72 per cent of all informants gave an alternative approximating to 'caggy-handed'. Three informants left the notion unanswered; however, they were quizzed about this at interview and revealed that they would use the standard notion, hence their data has been added to the data for the response 'left-handed'. What variation there is hinges here on the distinction between the use of the standard notion 'left-handed' and the alternatives 'caggy', 'caggy-handed' and 'cacky-handed'. Use of the standard notion is highest among the youngest informants at 50 per cent, and drops to 12.5 per cent in the 27–40 age group; it is not recorded at all for the 41–60 age group. In the 61–70 age group, levels of the standard notion are at 25 per cent, rising to 29 per cent for the 71+ age group (the number of informants in this group is seven). The appearance of 'cacky-handed' is only in the 16–26 age group. This may be a usage formed by analogy with the word 'cack', in common use in the Black Country for the standard 'faeces'. This ties in with comments made by two informants who were asked whether the phrase was insulting or not:

> INT 'What about left-handed?'INFa: 'Caggy-handed.' [Laughs]
> INT: 'Caggy-handed?'
> INFb: 'Yeah. I've got caggy-handed as well.'
> INT: 'Is it rude?'
> INFa: 'I [emphasis] think so yeah(.)not very nice is it?'
> INFb: 'I've got a brother who's left-handed(.)and he wouldn't be pleased at all if I used that.'

An informant in the 27–40 age group is less definite about the pejorative nature of the alternative, but her choice of words is telling: 'I have my knife and fork the wrong way round so I'm caggy-handed(.)it's just a term for somebody who does something(.)awkward(.)not the way it should be.'

As informants get older, so too does their use of the alternative 'caggy'. It is not reported at all by informants aged 16–26, but levels rise to 25 per cent for those aged 27–40, and rise again to 50 per cent for the age groups 41–60 and 61–70. They are highest at 57 per cent for the 71+ age group. This tallies with data from the corpus of dialect words. Walker (undated: 12) has 'caggy' for 'left-handed', but does not list 'caggy-handed'. Raven also lists only 'caggy' (1979: 8), and also remarks that it is 'used as a name for a left-handed person'. Older informants sometimes feel that the alternative 'caggy' does not carry pejorative overtones, but is simply a descriptive label. For example, discussion with an informant's older brother (who was seventy-five at the time of recording) exemplifies this well:

> INF: (*brother*) 'No, it ay offensive. Just caggy, and that's it.'
> INT: 'Caggy-handed?'
> INF: (*brother*) 'Even people that are caggy-handed will say, "I'm caggy handed"(.)It ay disrespectful to im, no.'

They also report that it is an epithet which can be used as a form of address for a person who is left-handed. For example, one informant remarked that it is possible to use the alternative as a directional; she related at interview a tale of asking for directions to a house, and the reply from the Gornal resident (one mile north-east of Dudley) she had asked was: 'You goes up here(.)and you turns caggy.'

The semantic overtones of the alternative 'caggy' are in dispute among informants. While many informants over seventy felt that the alternative carries no additional meaning of 'clumsy', younger ones reported that 'It's not quite the right thing to be.'

In conclusion then, there are two social forces at play in determining whether or not someone should be addressed with an alternative that is not 'left-handed'. Very elderly informants use the word 'caggy' as an epithet, and do not find it offensive. Over time, however, teachers learned more tolerance towards left-handed pupils, and what was once regarded as the norm – that left-handedness could mark a person out and was stamped out where possible – changed. This goes some way towards explaining the growing taboo associated with the alternatives 'caggy', 'cag-handed' and 'cak-handed'. In the same way as racism has become less tolerated (two of the oldest informants gave the phrase 'work like a black' for 'work hard', and insisted that this was not offensive), so persecution of left-handed children has dwindled, and with it has grown the taboo of marking these children and adults out as different.

4.2.5 Sweets

The most common alternative here, eliciting a response at the 64 per cent level for knowledge and/or use, was the local word 'suck'. Together with the closely related 'suckers', the two alternatives dominate. The standard 'sweets' is only reported at the 21 per cent level. On closer examination though, it can be deduced that some speakers do not use the word as frequently as they thought when they reflect on this at interview:

> INT: 'What do you call sweets?'
> INF 1: 'Suck(.)Well(.)I dunno(.)I sometimes call them sweets.'
> INF 6: 'Yeah, but suck's like.'
> INF 1: 'Rock and that.'
> INF 6: 'Yeah, candy(.)rock'
> INF 1: 'Yeah(.)them rock dummies and that.'
> INT: 'And would you use suck?'
> INF 1: 'Yeah(.)I dunno actually(.)maybe.'

The problem of asking informants for words they hear as well as words they use is again clear here. INF 2, for example, discussed the notion word 'stomach' later on in his interview, and gave the word 'gut' as his primary alternative; but when questioned at interview he said he would not use it, and that 'I was trying to give you something from the area like.' Informants do sometimes remark that they do not use the word they have written down on the sheet.

Bearing this in mind, if we break down the sample by age, we can see that informants in the 16–26 age group only give 'suck' as their primary alternative 37.5 per cent of the time. They are responsible for much of the variation in the sample: three informants respond with an alternative which is neither 'suck' nor 'sweets'. It is clear that younger speakers may be aware of the word, but do not use it at very high levels.

Reporting of 'suck' is highest at 87.5 per cent among the 41–60 and 61–70 age groups. It drops among the 71+ age group to 57 per cent. This fall among the oldest speakers in reporting the local alternative mirrors the fall in their reporting of the alternative 'lamp' for 'hit'. Two points come out of this finding. Lexically, the 71+ age group exhibit greater variation in their choice of lexis. The second, and related point, has to do with the comments made by Macafee (1994: 70) where he notes that 'the first process of lexical erosion . . . is the shift from active to passive knowledge'. Speakers under seventy in this study are sometimes keen to report alternatives which they know to be local, while being happy to tell the interviewer that they themselves might not use the word. On the other hand, speakers over seventy are more likely to be happier to report using different alternatives. The reasons for this are unclear. The desire to mark the knowledge of local variants appears to be stronger among those aged 27−60 than it does among older and younger people. It is certain that we may consider 'suck' to be a typical local variant, for Walker gives 'sucks' as meaning 'sweets' in his dictionary (undated: 34), and Beach (1998) gives the mass noun 'suck' as meaning 'sweets': 'candy to the Yanks, lollies to the Aussies'.

Chinn and Thorne's statement (2002: 10) that Birmingham and the Black Country have dialects which 'merge seamlessly into one another' is a sound one. It is not possible to find a word cited by informants which can be proven to be found only in Birmingham or only in the Black Country. INF 28 mentions 'spice'; she is from West Bromwich and has relatives from Birmingham. She clearly recalls not knowing the word on her first visits to her cousins. Chinn and Thorne do not, however, list the word 'spice', but they do list 'sucks' 'cuccuccs' and 'rocks' (2002: 153). INF 23 recalls his mother using 'cuckoo' in West Bromwich on the Birmingham border, which might suggest that the word and related alternatives have a Birmingham connection. INF 27, however, whose parents were born and raised in Upper Gornal (as she was) in the centre of the Black Country, also gives this word. It is true, however, that INF 23 gave 'rocks' as an alternative linked with Birmingham at interview:

INT: 'What do you call sweets?'
INF 23: 'Suck(.)rocks(.)My aunty comes from Handsworth in Birmingham and they always say "I bought you a bag of rocks"(.)but they always say rocks are not like chocolate.'

This would tally with 'rocks' being a possible shibboleth of Birmingham lexis. However, to claim that the alternative does not exist in the Black Country on the report of one informant would be inferring too much to be a scholarly conclusion.

In terms of agreed norms of usage and meaning, speakers are, for the most part, agreed that 'suck' is a mass noun − thus, 'some suck' is the correct phrase − and that 'suck' refers to boiled sweets, since they are the sweets that can be sucked. In a similar pattern to the age-related data examined above, three informants in the 16−26 age group, and one informant over seventy-one, include 'chocolate', 'pick and mix' and 'toffees' in their semantic range for what qualifies as sweets. Only one informant insisted that chocolate could be subsumed under the heading 'suck'. This is not enough evidence to disprove any theory that the agreed community norms surrounding what kind of food can count as 'suck' are anything but very strong indeed, particularly since INF 7 has parents who are from Worcester, and may have different norms. It is only INF 38 who gives 'suckers' for sweets, and if Walker's definition is representative of usage, the variants 'sucks' and 'suckers' coexist with 'suck'. There is not enough data to examine patterns of covariation, and it is in any case clear that 'suck' is the dominant term.

What can again be shown is the connection between self-declared social class and the retention of dialect lexis. Of twenty self-declared working-class and upper-working-class speakers, only two give the response 'sweets', and one 'confectionary', with sixteen giving 'suck' and one 'suckers'. Out of a total of fifteen lower-middle and middle-class speakers, only six give 'suck', with three giving 'sweets' and six giving other responses. It is the middle class who exhibit the most variation in their lexical choice, and the middle class who tend towards the standard usage.

4.2.6 Running Water Smaller than a River

The most common alternatives given here are 'brook' and 'stream'. It is clear from the data that there is both age patterning and semantic shift in progress. The age-related decline in the use of 'brook' and its replacement by 'stream' is obvious. Among younger speakers, just such a process is underway with the alternative 'brook'. One informant, aged 24, articulates this well: 'Erm, there's a place called "the brook" by my house(.)which is just a stream. Everyone calls it "the brook"(.)but I don't think I'd say it apart from to talk about that place.'

Another informant called the stretch of running water near her house 'the brook', but was certain that she only used the alternative for this one stretch of water. In the older age groups it is also possible to see this process at work. As further evidence of 'brook' becoming more restricted in meaning, we can cite evidence from speakers who list different conditions for something being a 'brook'. One informant, forty-seven at the time of recording, remarks that: 'Probably a brook is smaller than a stream.' Another, also forty-seven at the time of recording, sets out a hierarchy of size, commenting that 'A brook's smaller than a stream and a stream is smaller than a river.' They are not the only informants to set conditions for terming something a 'brook', as the following extract shows:

> INF: 'Like running water smaller than a river I put like "stream" and "brook".'
> INT: 'Which one is smaller?'
> INF: 'Oh that's(.)I'd say brook(.)a brook always for me is paired up with bubbling(.)which for me(.)just like running over things(.)not a permanent fixture(.)a stream would be like a permanent fixture and a brook possibly wouldn't be.'

In conclusion, we can see that the preferred alternative for running water smaller than a river is changing over time as allegiances shift from 'brook' to 'stream'. The word 'brook' is becoming restricted and fossilised, preserved in specific place names. This is not to say that the process will complete rapidly – three informants under forty listed 'brook' as their secondary alternative, and the word is still widely known. Not one of the informants claimed that they had never heard the word. That said, the evidence presented here shows that we may reasonably hypothesise that use of the alternative 'brook' will continue to decline in the Black Country.

4.2.7 Dog

We look now at information gathered about the alternative [waml] for dog. Walker (undated: 2) claims that this derives from 'mongrel – from OE [hwæmelec]'. This etymology cannot be found in any of the standard reference texts on Anglo-Saxon lexis; indeed, repeated attempts during this study failed to trace its origin. Chinn and Thorne (2002: 163) also list the word for Birmingham use as: 'wammal n. mongrel; an animal, especially a dog, of a mixed breed . . . also common in the Black Country dialect'.

Beach spells the word 'wammel', and gives it a gloss of 'dog'. These three explanations are not preceded by earlier references; however, the earlier sources of dialect are considerably shorter in length than the later sources listed here, and concentrate for the most part on adjectives describing people and things, rather than on nouns. In our own data, the major alternative listed for 'dog' is simply the standard 'dog'. Fifty-six per cent of informants give this as their primary response, and 10 per cent list 'mutt' as the primary alternative. Only 13 per cent give 'wammal', since the other 21 per cent give responses of 'bow-wow', 'pooch', 'mongrel', 'hound' and 'fido'.

Looking more closely at the reports of 'wammal', we can add in secondary alternatives. Of the informants who give 'dog' as their primary alternative, two give the secondary response 'wammal'. One informant, whose primary response is 'mongrel', lists 'scrammal' as his secondary alternative. We return to the question of 'scrammal' and its place in the system of names for dogs presently. Collating all informants who gave 'wammal' as a response, it can be seen that no one in the 16–26 age group lists the alternative at all. In the 27–40 age group two informants list 'wammal' and one 'scrammal'; in the 41–60 age group one informant lists the alternative; in the 61–70 age group three informants list it; and in the 71+ age group one informant lists it.

The pejorative nature of the word reinforces the definition given by Chinn and Thorne that the word means a 'mongrel'. Informants do not report that the word can be used for a pedigree dog, and, when reminded of the word, report that it would be used to chastise a dog if it were in the way. Though the term is friendly enough if used for one's own dog, informants who knew the word agreed that it was impolite for other dogs, and not a term of praise.

This lexical alternative is of interest also in that it introduces the related term 'scrammal'. One informant reports hearing the word 'scrammal' for a dog on her interview sheet, while the boyfriend of one informant, like her, in the 27–30 age group, also gives 'scrammal', but reports this at interview as meaning 'any small animal' (hamsters were one example he gave, dogs being too large). Information related to Rock (1974: 11) in Quarry Bank by her informants (all over sixty years old), suggests that they would discipline children for 'trapping a wammle (small animal)'. For other informants, such as one in the 16–26 age group, 'scrammal' equated with 'wammal' and carried the same semantic overtones. He explains: you couldn't turn round to a pedigree and say like(.)it's a scrammal'.

It is dangerous to hypothesise that shift is in progress one way or the other in the face of a lack of diachronic evidence. It may be that two competing (and semantically allied) meanings have existed for a long time. Some informants have begun a process of fossilisation of the word, restricting it to one particular dog, while others are busy actively using it. Furthermore, others use an alternative form 'scrammal' to represent the same concept of 'dog', and some use 'scrammal' for the semantically related category of small animals. Clearly the process Macafee describes does not always flow as neatly as do the examples given in her framework. The status of both 'wammal' and 'scrammal' is not clear, but both are known by some within the speech community, and being semantically related, there is overlap in their meaning and use for different speakers. The two alternatives are a good example of lexical semantic norms in dispute within a community.

4.2.8 Conclusions

It may be the case, as Trudgill (1999: 20) points out, that many dialect words are gradually disappearing from English, especially as a consequence of rural lifestyle changes and modern dialects replacing traditional dialects. To some extent, lexis in Birmingham and the Black Country is indeed subject to the changes Trudgill outlines. For example, data from the project discussed here showed that there is attrition in the use of the term 'brook' for running water smaller than a river. We have seen that some speakers are less likely to use the word 'suck' for 'sweets'. What we have also seen, however, is that lexical attrition among the words looked at closely is slow to take place. The stable norms governing the use of the word 'suck' show us that speakers still have a consensus about what the word constitutes, and that they know which sweets can be 'suck'. Conversely, the fact that the oldest age group of 71+ show variation in what they allow to come under the semantic heading of 'suck' might suggest that we should be cautious in attributing all lexical change to the younger age groups. Since it is the older group who claim that 'sucks' and 'suckers' (in other words count nouns) are acceptable terms for 'sweets', we might look at the development of the word 'sucks' in a different light, and claim that the shift from 'suckers' to 'suck' took place some time ago, so that what looks like an established traditional alternative for 'sweets' may in fact be the newer traditional alternative.

It would not be sensible to claim that all variation is being lost, or that no new variation is coming into Birmingham and the Black Country. The existence of the alternative 'twag' for telling tales on someone shows this well. It has apparently come into the local variety relatively recently, since older informants were capable of remembering their own childhood alternatives for the concept, which include 'telltale twit', 'sneak' and 'snitch', but did not know 'twag', even when prompted at interview. It is reasonable to claim that there is indeed new growth in the lexical inventory of the local variety with the arrival of this alternative.

On a related matter, the survival of the alternative 'wammal' might, at first sight, be viewed as a good example of a word being restricted to 'narrower and narrower functions' (Trudgill 1990: 20). It is clear, on closer inspection, that its coexistence with the related alternative 'scrammal' makes for a more complex situation. Speakers cannot be completely clear about whether 'wammal' and 'scrammal' both mean dog, or whether 'scrammal' can mean any small animal. In some way this lack of agreed norms accounts for the marginal survival of both alternatives. 'Scrammal' is not becoming restricted as 'wammal' is among some speakers, and it is possible that its future may be healthier than that of 'wammal'.

The preservation of certain items of local lexis by the self-declared working class is an interesting phenomenon which may tally with their social mobility. Trudgill (1999: 21) reports that the retention of the term 'squit' for 'nonsense' in Norwich has been possible because it is now used by speakers 'informally, maybe jokingly, and is therefore not necessarily in competition with Standard English words such as nonsense which can be used in more formal situations'. This does not, however, explain the reporting of the alternative 'lamp' at high levels by working-class speakers in the sample for this project. It is surely not in dispute that they have at their command the standard item 'hit', yet they report 'lamp'. If, as Trudgill suggests, they can use this word jocularly, with 'hit' being used in more formal situations, then why do the self-declared middle class not use it? The answer may lie in the lack of transmission of local words among the middle class, which might reasonably be linked to their weaker social connections with the area and their greater social mobility. But it may equally be linked to a desire to avoid such words, for some informants at interview laugh at local words and claim that they have overtones of being just that – local, with which they do not wish to be associated.

4.3 The West Midlands Dialect Project

The source of the data given below comes from recordings made between 2001 and 2007, conducted with both male and female informants aged between twenty-four and eighty-four years. Chapter 1 has discussed the methodology of this research project, with data collected by undergraduate students. The five interviews discussed in more detail here have been selected on the basis of showing the greatest degree of lexical variation. The three male informants were aged nineteen, twenty-four, and seventy-three, with two female informants aged thirty-one and eighty-three. It is clear that, in everyday conversation, speakers tend to use a mixture of lexis, comprising: a) Standard English items, b) items variant from Standard English which also occur in regions beyond Birmingham and the Black Country, and c) lexis specific to the region. Items which also occur in regions beyond Birmingham and the Black Country, and throughout the interviews discussed – such as 'chap' for 'man', 'nan' for 'grandmother', 'brassic' for 'broke' (when referring to money), and 'a walkover' for something that is easy to do – are not discussed here. The figure below shows the items that occurred most frequently.

Of the five interviews, two produced the greatest degree of lexical variation; one was from a female aged thirty-one and the other from a male aged seventy-four. The younger informant, a white female, had been born in West Bromwich, then moved to Langley via Whiteheath, with all three areas coming under the Borough of Sandwell. This interview centred on an nurse using the SuRE method:

> INT: 'And what would you say to your friends if they're going on too much?'
> INF: 'They're gassing too much. They're babbling on and on. Things like that has gas babble babble "canting" – too much "canting".'
> *and*
> INF: 'Hard work you call "graft". Working, working your tripe out. That's right, not to use your left hand you'd call "caggy-handed" . . . When I was a kid, small streams you would call a "brook".'

The informant, a white male aged seventy-four, had lived all his life in Walsall. The recording here centred on a sociolinguistic interview. The extracts below contextualise the lexical items in Figure 4.3. The first extract below shows how 'All around the Wrekin' is used metaphorically to talk about the length of a long journey, and 'Like watching a coffin warp' in relation to his gardening skills:

> INF: 'Like, if you wanted to go from here to, er, Stafford Street, you've got to stop and think. Well Wolverhampton Road you've got to stop and think "Which is best?" I've got to go down and meet them now . . . whereas before, I used to go just under the subway second on the right along Marsh Street out on to the Tipton Wolverhampton Road by the Savoy, but now you've got to go all around the Wrekin to get anywhere.'
> *and*
> INT: 'So, it's Josianne who does the garden then. Not you?'
> INF: 'No. I'm useless up the garden. It's like watching a coffin warp.'

The lexical item 'cut' is often used in place of the word 'canal', as the following extract shows:

> INT: 'That's a lie. Can you sow mars? Yes, I would sow an overcoat on this button.'

Item (Black Country)	Function and Standard English equivalent
named	verb: 'was named' as opposed to: 'was called'
lezzer	noun: 'meadow'
bit	noun: 'wait a bit' as opposed to: 'wait a moment'
cut	noun: 'canal'
goosegog	noun: 'gooseberry'
baggies	noun: West Bromwich Albion football supporter
stop	verb: 'stop and have a cup of tea' as opposed to 'stay and have a cup of tea'
canting	verb: 'talking' – usually gossip, and associated with women
clammed	verb: 'hungry'
brook	noun: 'small stream'
caggy-handed	noun: 'left-handed'
(Phrases)	
A time or two	Once or twice
All around the Wrekin	Circumlatory talk
Like watching a coffin warp	Something that is boring to watch
Wait a bit	Wait a moment

Figure 4.3 Lexical Items

> INF: 'Ar, and the other kid who was fishing up the cut, he says "Me mates fell into the cut".'

One male informant, aged nineteen, had lived in Willenhall all his life. There is a good deal of rivalry in this area between the football teams Wolverhampton Wanderers (Wolves) and West Bromwich Albion (The Baggies). He said: 'I thought that we'd have a good go and maybe we'd do it, but I wouldn't be too downhearted if we get relegated as long as The Baggies don't come up.'

Unlike its meaning in Standard English, 'wench' – meaning 'girl' (usually older usage) maintains no pejorative overtones in Black Country usage, and is found in a number of interviews across the span of data.

> INF: *(female, 25)* 'I shared a room with this wench called Julie. She was a bit younger – she was eighteen. Eighteen or nineteen; I can't remember. But she was really nice.'
> INF: *(male, 56)* 'I use the word "wench" a lot. I wouldn't use it with outside women because they'd take offence . . . but my girls call each other "wenches" and the friends do.'

The lexical item 'babby' is common in Birmingham and the Black Country in place of Standard English 'baby'. It is also used in households to refer to the youngest child, and appears frequently across the data.

> INF: *(female 25)* 'The second time she was pregnant with a babby.'
> INF: *(female 28)* 'Our babby was twelve-month old.'
> INF: *(female 29)* 'They're like fourteen having a babby . . . and then the babby gets to thirteen and has a babby.'
> INF: *(female 56)* 'I can remember women standing outside, a babby in one arm and a pint of beer in the other.'
> INF: *(male 56)* 'You know I want every babby to be able to get on, and they can only get on if they have access to Standard English.'

Lexical items found more specifically in areas of the Black Country, and across informants of all ages, include:
'day' for Standard English 'didn't':

> INF: 'Because they've got languages what he day do.'
> INF: 'I day go in until the Monday.'
> INF: 'Joe day come the same time as me, he came on his own.'

'ay' for Standard English 'aren't' or 'haven't':

> INF: 'It ay him is it I mean, he's always been that independent ay he and that's his trouble.'
> INF: 'And it's dangerous ay it?'

'cor' for Standard English 'can't':

> INF: He says I don't know I cor remember.
> INF: Well at eighteen I cor stop him anyway.

'doh' for Standard English 'don't':

>   INF: 'Go if yam a going, doh stop.'
>   INF: 'And then you have two years doh you?'
>   INF: 'If we do, we do, if we doh, we doh.'

'am' for Standard English 'are':

>   INF: 'Mark's convinced we're having twins. Yeah right, one of them's going back if we am.'
>   INF: 'It doesn't matter where you am in the country.'

'yam' or 'youm' for Standard English 'you are':

>   INF: 'Go if yam a going.'
>   INF: 'And then the kids start wailing at you and youm like, "Well what can I do about it?"'

'ar' [ɑː] is the usual Black Country word for 'yes' and is extremely common among all age groups. Instances of less frequently occurring Birmingham and Black Country lexical items include:
'blarting' for Standard English 'crying':

>   INF: 'If I go to Castle Vale or Shard End the kids will understand what I mean if I say "Pack up your blarting".'

'robble' for Standard English 'tangle up':

>   INF: 'How you'd get your stockings in a robble over me.'

and 'miskin' for Standard English 'waste tip':

>   INF: 'My old man never calls the dustbin "the dustbin". He calls it "the miskin".'

4.4 Language and Place: Birmingham and Language, Performance and Region – Discourse and Sociocultural Identity in the Black Country

This section discusses the most commonly featured lexical items and phrases used by performers and prominent people associated with the Birmingham and Black Country region as they occurred in interview. For example, the lexical item 'Brummie' is rife across interlocutors, highlighting the magnitude of its usage. During an interview with Malcolm Stent, a Birmingham based playwright, it is used as a somewhat divergent utterance dispelling any confusion and accentuating an emblematic 'Brummie' identity – taking ownership of identity:

> INF: 'And a lot of people hear me speak and they say, "Because you're from the Black Country"; and I say, "No I'm not. I'm not from the Black Country. I'm a . . . I'm a Brummie."'
> INT: 'It's usually the other way around?'
> INF: 'Yeah, and . . . and people get er, you know, get very angry and rightly so, er, people from the Black Country when they're mistaken for Brummies.'

Vernacular forms such as 'Brummie gems' and 'Brummagem' are also incorporated and maintained:

> INF: 'In the past, Hatton Garden always looked down on Birmingham's Jewellery Quarter. And things that came from our Jewellery Quarter were considered second class – they weren't – and they were considered inferior and they were called "Brummie gems". And, and, you know, that's where, er, the nickname "Brummagem" comes from.'

Phrases such as 'on a line' meaning 'angry' are maintained within a colloquial lexicon:

> INF: 'My mum were off on a line.'

A plethora of the 'Brummie' usage is mirrored across interviews and performances indexing locality. For example, a Birmingham performer said in interview:

> INF: 'Over the years I've adapted the way I speak according to . . . like when I was at university I had to tone it down. Erm, when I'm with my family they're all Brummies. They're not Black Country people, they're Brummies. So it's different then.'

Lexical demonyms such as 'Midlander' or 'West Midlander' which pertain to originating from this locality are employed, and thus evident in performer interviews across Birmingham:

> INF: 'Erm, I don't know why that is really. Just I think Midlanders are, so I think that, generally, Midlanders associate . . . West Midlanders associate themselves more with northerners than southerners.'

Lexical clippings are prevalent by truncating Standard English forms, one pertinent to Birmingham and the Black Country being 'baby'. Variations include 'babby' and 'bab':

> INF: 'Yes, yes . . . and, er, he never says "baby" he says "babby" all the time.'
> INF: 'Yes . . . "bab, bab, bab" all the time. I, I, I, I make an effort to reintroduce "bab" whenever I can, and now loads of my friends that are not even from Birmingham, they all say it.'

As already mentioned above, forms which are used beyond Birmingham and the Black Country are also nurtured and preserved in this locality, 'nan' being one of them:

> INF: 'But my, my, nan fell out with her dad because her mom died and within a year he'd married this other woman next door neighbour who my nan hated. And she said if you marry her I'm never going to speak to you again.'

Data from both the social historian Carl Chinn and the actor Julie Walters shows that, lexically, the words 'Brummie' for someone who hails from Birmingham, 'bab' or 'babs' for a girl or young women, and 'wench', also for a women, are still in use. Julie states: 'I loved the fact I was called 'bab'. I thought that was my name till I was about fourteen.' As Carl Chinn points out, the word 'bab' derives from the Anglo-Saxon 'babby': '"bab", my girls would call their mates when they talk to each other — "wench" or "bab", particularly "bab"'. From Carl Chinn's interview, it is clear that the term 'blarting' for 'crying' is still very much in use. He remarks: 'My nan would never say "crying"; it would be "blarting" . . . you know, if I go to Castle Vale or Shard End the kids understand what I mean if I say "Pack up your blarting" . . .'

These three words in particular — 'Brummie', 'bab' or 'babs', and 'wench' appear to survive any kind of lexical attrition and have instead become enregistered or emblematic of contemporary Birmingham dialect, as too, has the word 'Brummie'. A Birmingham Poet Laureate, Spoz, describes how, when he is performing poetry outside Birmingham — in London or Manchester — he emphasises his Birmingham accent, as the following extract shows:

> Spoz: 'I really start emphasising the Brummyism because I want people to know, I want people to know that's where I'm from.'
> INT: 'And do you find if you travel off the region you can get some flak?'
> Spoz: 'Very much so, yes, ar.'

INT: 'And you feed off that?'

Spoz: 'Yes, I do. I'm, I really ... although having said that I did a thing up in Manchester recently and, erm, there seems to be a camaraderie amongst regional accent speakers whatever your regional accent happens to be.'

Spoz goes on to report that this camaraderie has no North–South divide, but is instead based on a more personal realisation of place.

One lexical item which has become emblematic of the Black Country region is 'bostin', although it is often used in Birmingham. Spoz says:

'Now we're talking sort of south, south Birmingham Rubery I suppose. The closest, Halesowen ... we aren't far from Halesowen which is just sneaking into the Black Country isn't it. And I had this t-shirt – I was doing a gig with Attila the Stockbroker actually – and I had this t-shirt with "bostin" and he had no idea what it meant, so I'm explaining oh "bostin", it's a Brummie/ Black Country kind of word which means "really good" – you know, "great". And there was this guy from Dudley who went "Oi mate, it ay a Brummie word it's a Black Country word." I goes, 'Excuse me mate, don't get sancti-monious with me.'

West Bromwich is a former town (now part of Birmingham) forming a border with the Black Country – a border which is difficult to define in geographic terms. The poet Geoff Stevens, who came from West Bromwich, used to perform a poem called *Grandad's Night Out*:

It was the day before my grandad's 90th birthday
And he'd been saying there wasn't anywhere exciting to go at night
For blokes getting on a bit as he was
And then I saw in a local paper
Bromwich nightclub to hold 80s and 90s evenings starting tonight at 10 o'clock
So I thought that's a 'bostin' idea so I took him along
This 7 foot black man in a suit was on the door and he said
Where you going with him
And I said in there and he say you aye he's too old
He'll be a safety risk a danger to himself
But you advertised it as an 80s and 90s night and he's over 80
Well smart arse he said well its 90s night tonight and the 80s night is next week.

This poem could refer to any man anywhere in the country approach-ing his ninetieth birthday and his grandson looking for ways to help him celebrate it. However, through phonology, syntax and, particularly in this case, lexis, the verbal pun on 80s and 90s music with chronological age is regionalised lexically through the item 'bostin'.

Mick Pearson, the editor of *The Black Countryman*, points to a greater identification with specific localities within the Black Country than within Birmingham. He says: 'The difference for me is, if you're in Birmingham – let's say you come from Aston, in Birmingham. Would you call yourself an Astonian? Would you call yourself a Brummie? I think people would say "I come from Birmingham" first; whereas in the Black Country, "Oh, I'm from Netherton." "Where's Netherton?" "It's in the – oh, it's in the Black Country."'

Al Atkins, the rock musician, speaks of a time when a translation had to be made when making conversation over a meal with his future brother-in-law, who came from Kent. When the meal finished, his future brother-in-law asked Al where he was going. Al said: 'I said . . . I always remember saying it, and he fell about on the floor laughing. I said 'We're going rot, we're going rotting up the cut.' And my sister said 'They're going rottin up. They're going to catch rats up the canal.'

Al also talks about the men in his family, who worked at a steelworks. As a child, he would look through the bars of the factory gates where you could see 'the hot "gleeds" falling out everywhere'. Lexis, such as 'gleeds' and 'brewuss' for 'wash house' and 'sough' for 'drain', although remembered by Atkins and Chinn, seem to be lost to contemporary generations.

It would seem then that, for certain types of performers – for their performances and the audiences who come to watch them – identification with a region through use of accent and dialect is very much a part of their act. The data from the two Language, Performance and Place projects, with regards to lexis, seem to indicate that certain words used in Birmingham and the Black Country – not thought by speakers to be any different from any other part of the country – have, through processes of indexicalisation, become enregistered or marked as emblematic of the region. Thus, to mark themselves as 'Brummie' or 'Black Country', one of the resources upon which speakers draw self-consciously is the use of regionally 'marked' or emblematised lexis which is also recognised as such by their audience.

4.5 Conclusion

The data discussed in this chapter, collected as part of various projects, shows clearly that there are lexical items which are shared between the two communities, but also that there are distinct differences. There is evidence that certain words and phrases 'belong' to Birmingham, others to the Black Country, and others still to them both. The term 'babs' for a women, for example, is perceived widely as a Birmingham dialect word, whereas 'bostin' is associated with the Black Country, although also heard in Birmingham. Across the data as a whole, it is clear that the lexical items 'cut' for 'canal' and 'caggy-handed' for 'left-handed' – and used as a pejorative term – are still in use today in everyday speech.

What the data discussed in this chapter show, especially in section 4.4, is that certain lexical items are drawn upon, along with phonological and morphosyntactic items discussed in Chapters 2 and 3, to 'mark' or enregister 'Brummie' or 'Black Country' both to local audiences and those further afield. This chapter also shows, especially in section 4.2, that although lexical attrition has taken place due to changes in industrial practices once associated with the region, lexical difference still occurs. In addition, the data discussed in sections 4.3 and 4.4 demonstrate how specific lexical items are being used by performers self-consciously, in a more iconic or enregistered way, as emblematic of the region to which they refer. Lexical features associated with the region are consciously chosen and employed through performative acts such as comic and dramatic performance.

5 Survey of Previous Works and Bibliography

5.1 An Overview of Linguistic Research Concerning Birmingham and Black Country English

Birmingham and Black Country English are both typical of varieties situated on the so-called North–South linguistic divide in England. In both morphological and phonological terms it sits on this boundary, or to be more precise, forms a transition zone which might more reasonably be termed a 'Midlands' dialect area.

5.1.1 Birmingham English

Wells's 1982 work on accents of English in the British Isles includes a description of what he terms 'West Midlands phonology'. Although this work gives a good overview of possible phonological variation in the regional variety, very little previous work has been undertaken on Birmingham English, which remains an under-researched area. The lack of purely linguistic research concerning Birmingham is possibly a reflection on the low status accorded to urban varieties as essentially bastardised and corrupted dialects, not seen as pure and correct forms of dialect with a historical pedigree.

The first sources available to any linguistic investigation from linguists themselves come from Ellis (1889) and his large-scale survey of phonological variation in the British Isles. Ellis visited one location in Birmingham, this being Selly Oak. As what was by then an urban locality, the city was passed over by the *Survey of English Dialects* (*SED*) with its emphasis on questioning non-mobile, older, rural males. Since the main aims of the *SED* were philological and historical, attempting to catalogue earlier lexical variation and the preservation of older phonological and morphological variation among older rural males, Birmingham was not seen as a suitable ground for linguistic investigation. The nearest location to the city of Birmingham was the

Warwickshire town of Hockley Heath, eleven miles to the south-east. Reference to this source does however show that the variety spoken in Hockley Heath has much in common with that now spoken in the city of Birmingham itself. The most comprehensive source in recent years is Thorne (2003). The major focus of Thorne's research was investigating attitudes to stigmatised urban varieties in the UK, focusing on his hometown of Birmingham. In conducting this research, Thorne sets out a comprehensive account of Birmingham English in structural linguistic terms, so as to be able to focus on the variables which are remarked on as stigmatised within Birmingham and without. Thorne gives examples of regularisation using weak suffixes such as 'I knowed him a long time ago' and 'I've knowed 'er since 'er was a nipper.' He gives examples of regularisation to the past participial form such as 'well, a chap [sɪn] me 'avin' a fight in the street', and 'the reason they done that was . . .'. He also gives the example, 'if I'd 'ave give up my 'ome I couldn't take anything of my own with me'. Thorne also reports that the letter 'a' has phonological variants ranging from [a] to [ə], regularly added as a prefix in the speech of older working-class Brummies to the present participle of verbs such as 'come', 'go', 'walk', 'play', 'stand', 'tell' and 'knock. This use is also evident in the past or present continuous tenses – for example, 'You en't a-tellin' me what to have!'

In the same way, Tennant (1982: 19) gives the example 'oimagunna' for what he glosses as 'I am going to', and (1982: 25) 'wuzzagunna' for 'I did intend to' or 'I was intending to.' He gives the example 'Oi wuzzagunna gew today but oi intagunna gew till tomorra – then oi amagunna gew fuddeffinit' (1982: 26). It seems likely from the evidence given that this feature is recessive within the city of Birmingham, and indeed, in the neighbouring Black Country.

Thorne's linguistic description draws together sources from across time, as well as original data gathered from several working-class speakers in Birmingham. He also focuses on eye-dialect literature. By eye-dialect, we understand the term to mean the phenomenon Matthews (2007: 134) describes as 'conventional misspellings of words, as e.g. <wuz> for [wəz], intended to suggest non-standard accents'.

Khan's 2006 research in Birmingham added to the existing canon of information. Crucially, his focus on ethnicity and language variation in the city added much to what is known about the interplay between the traditional Birmingham English and the newer variants associated with (but by no means necessarily the preserve of) certain ethnic groups.

5.1.2 Black Country English

In 1982, Wells's influential three volume *Accents of English* series was published. The popularity of the volumes has meant that the two sources he used for the Black Country have led many to extrapolate 'firm' conclusions, which they consider to have been arrived at by Wells himself, concerning the phonological system of the region, from a very small (and considerably dated) amount of evidence. Wells's lexical sets feature in Asprey's 2007 analysis of phonology and in Chapter 2 of this book, with examination running much deeper than does his. Chapter 3 of this book aside, morphology and syntax can only be said to have been covered in serious detail by Manley (1971) and Higgs (2004).

Major sources, beginning with the earliest, are as follows. A. J. Ellis (1889) collected data, primarily phonological, from Bradley, 'Cannock Chase' (the exact location of the informant is unclear), Codsall, Cradley, Darlaston, Dudley, Enville, Stourbridge, Walsall, Wednesbury, West Bromwich, Willenhall and Wolverhampton. He found a split between varieties which runs through the southern Black Country. Indeed, his linguistic definition of the region also uses regional labels, and he splits down two varieties:

> Var. ii*b*, The 'Black Country' of South Staffordshire [this covers Walsall, Willenhall, Wolverhampton, Darlaston, and Dudley]

> Var. ii*c*, north Worcestershire – Near Black Country proper [this covers Cradley, Stourbridge, Selly Oak and Hagley] (1889: 485)

Since Ellis allowed others to write down samples of language and send them in, care must be taken in relying on this data, although it is transcribed to a high level of detail.

Gibson (1955) collected data for the *Survey of English Dialects* (*SED*) in Himley, in the extreme south of the Black Country (lying 0.75 miles west of Gornal). One informant was subsequently recorded by Stanley Ellis. Gibson interviewed three informants – two male, one female, and all of them over sixty. It is interesting to note that there are only two locations in or near the Black Country covered by the *SED*. In Figure 5.1, Himley is shown marked by \11 in County 11, which is Salop (a local term for Shropshire). Today, it would be considered as part of the Black Country, and indeed, Parsons (1986) considers Himley to be part of the Black Country. The next location closest is the village of Romsley, marked \1 in County 16, Worcestershire. It is never mentioned in any description as lying within the Black Country, yet lies only 2.5 miles south-west of Halesowen, and would today be considered

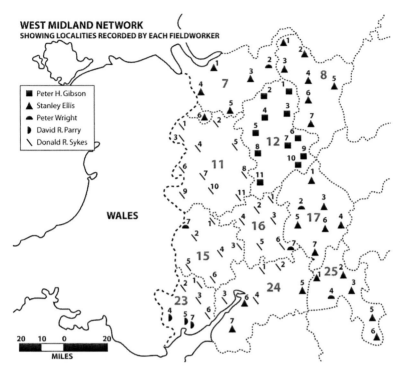

Figure 5.1 West Midland Localities in the *Survey of English Dialects* (Orton and Barry 1969)

as being in the Black Country or on the border of the Black Country. County 12 is Staffordshire, and County 17 is Warwickshire. With the exception of Warwickshire, today's Black Country is made up of joining and neighbouring areas within Counties 11, 12 and 16 – namely Shropshire (Salop), Staffordshire and Worcestershire. So the lack of any physically defined region known as 'The Black Country' means its borders remain a continued source of contestation.

In 1963, Painter collected a small amount of phonological and morphological data from a darts match at the Red Lion pub in Rowley Regis in the present-day borough of Sandwell. There were three male informants, observed covertly in free conversation. This small study is cited by Wells (1982b). The other study Wells refers to is Heath (1971, 1980). The latter collected solely phonological data from the Cannock Urban District (now part, once more, of the wider County of Stafford). The study population comprised eighty informants from the areas of Pye Green, Cannock, Hednesford, Chadsmoor, Hazel Slade and Cannock

Wood. The Black Country lies to the south, beginning some six miles beyond Pelsall. The study is heavily cited by Wells (1982b: 364) as being representative of the 'Birmingham–Wolverhampton' phonological system, and, he adds, of 'the Black Country around Wolverhampton'. Examination of Heath's biodata shows that there was still in-migration at the start of the 1960s from the Black Country (Dudley for example) by miners seeking work. It is clear that the Cannock accent has features in common with the Black Country; some of these arose, however, comparatively recently, and possibly as a result of linguistic contact during mass in-migration. In diachronic dialectological terms, Cannock is also allied with the varieties of north and mid-Staffordshire. To use Heath's work as a source for the Black Country is wholly inappropriate.

The first more recent source of phonological and morphological information comes from Manley (1971). She collected anecdotes about working life in the south of the Black Country from eight informants in free conversation. In addition, one further female informant was asked to 'translate' verb paradigms from Standard English. The eight primary informants were all male, from Colley Gate, Cradley Heath, Halesowen and Lye in the borough of Dudley. As most are listed as retired, we could infer that they were over sixty-five. Manley looked chiefly at the verb system, and at phonology.

Mathisen (1999) worked on data collected from fifty-seven informants. The sample is stratified by class, gender and age. She used the Labovian framework of word-list style, through formality levels to conversational style. Informants came from Wednesbury, Tipton and Rowley Regis in the borough of Sandwell.

In 2004, Higgs published the results of a large survey in the south of the region – again in the borough of Dudley (specifically, in Dudley, Kingswinford, Brierley Hill and Wordsley). He concentrates on morphology, and his work, looking as it does at stylistic variation and the effect of interlocutor on choice of verb forms, is consistently thorough. His is the most comprehensive and reliable source on Black Country grammar at the present time.

Unlike the situation concerning the phonology and grammar of the language varieties found in the Black Country, there exists a large number of texts concerning the lexis of the area. Most offer a diachronic perspective, but some are more recent. Serious and scholarly studies of local lexis have been carried out by interested residents and visitors, and some by those who are linguists by profession.

Finally, much older historical data concerning phonological reflexes can be found in the *Linguistic Atlas of Late Mediaeval English* (McIntosh et al. 1986). There is also the *Vernon Manuscript*, discussed in Chapter 1, which contains over 350 Middle English texts, written c.1390–1400. This manuscript is written in the dialect spoken in the English West Midlands, and includes an extensive collection of poetry and prose for pious readers.

5.2 Literary, Folk and other Collections

A plentiful source of information comes also from written texts designed to try to reflect regional phonological and morphological systems, as well as to display local lexis, using standard orthographic conventions. Known variously as eye-dialect, respellings or regionalisms (Beal 2005), these texts attempt to capture regional variation in terms that the lay person, unversed in the International Phonetic Alphabet, can understand. Such texts are also typically self-referential, in that the intended audience is people who live in the Birmingham and Black Country regions, or are associated with it by birth, for example. In recent years, with the creation of institutions such as the Black Country Society and The Black Country Living Museum, the number of such texts has increased. Some of these contain much original material; others are clearly imitations of earlier publications. This caveat acknowledged, the texts can be useful in determining words perceived by the community as localised. Lexical sources range from Poole (1880), through Shaw (1930), on to Wilson (1974). More modern sources include dialect dictionaries (see Beach 1998; Parker 1984, 1991; Raven 1979; Wilson 1974), and translations of the Old Testament (Fletcher 1975).

Another source of information to which one can refer for lexis is the large number of song books which exist in the area. Institutions, such as the Wolverhampton Folk Song Club, have long had an interest in recording the traditional folk songs of the area. Many of these refer to local customs and events, such as wakes, fairs, bull baitings, cockfights and wife sales. Some also deal with political and social issues, such as the treatment of workers in mines, Chartism in the area, and the difficulties faced by those dealing with poor financial conditions and safety at work. The use of such song lyrics requires recognition that they refer to events which happened up to 200 years ago and more. They may contain fossilised features, or have been collected from singers whose region of origin is not known. That said, collectors do state that they went to considerable trouble to gather the lyrics from local people (the provenance of a song, and the person who taught you that song, are important parts of the wider culture of folk music). Within the limitations outlined, songs form a good source of lexical items. Research on the grammar of the Black Country is, if anything, even sparser. Songbooks contain much information on morphology over time.

5.3 Works Cited in this Chapter and the Book as a Whole

Agha, A. (2003), 'The social life of cultural value', *Language and Communication*, 23: 231–73.

Agha, A. (2007), *Language and Social Relations*, Cambridge: Cambridge University Press.

Anon (1981), 'Teachers need lessons … off Aynuk', *Express and Star*, 5 September 1981.

Asprey, E. (2001), 'A study in West Midland phonological variables', unpublished MA dissertation, University of Leeds.

Asprey, E. (2007), 'Black Country English and Black Country Identity', unpublished PhD dissertation, University of Leeds.

Bartlett, F. (1886), 'The Collier's Story – A tale of hard times', in F. Bartlett, *Flashes from Forge and Foundry*, Bilston: Shakespeare Printing Co.

BBC Voices Black Country (2005), 'Have your say', <http://www.bbc.co.uk/blackcountry/have_your_say/accents/accents.shtml> (last accessed 14 September 2006).

BBC Voices Birmingham (2005), 'Have your say', <http://www.bbc.co.uk/birmingham/voices2005/have_your_say.shtml> (last accessed 14 September 2006).

BBC Voices wordmaps (2005), 'BBC Voices wordmaps – selected theme: What you do; selected concept: to play truant', <http://www.bbc.co.uk/voices/results/wordmap/> (last accessed 21 March 2005).

Beach, I. (1998), '"Ow we spake" (Black Country Dialect)', <http://www.sedgleymanor.com/dictionaries/dialect.html> (last accessed 1 April 2005).

Beal, J. (2000), 'From Geordie Ridley to Viz: Popular Literature in Tyneside English', *Language and Literature*, 9: 343–59.

Beal, J. (2005), 'Dialect representation in texts', in K. Brown (ed.), *The Encyclopedia of Language and Linguistics*, 2nd edn, Oxford: Elseveier, pp. 531–8.

Beal, J. C. (2006), *Language and Region*, London: Routledge.

Beal, J. C. (2009), 'Enregisterment, commodification and historical context: "Geordie" versus "Sheffieldish"', *American Speech*, 84: 138–56.

Benham, C. (1890), 'Them Harnted Housen', reproduced by Foxearth and District Local History Society, <http://www.foxearth.org.uk/blog/2005_01_01_BlogArchive.html> (last accessed 15 September 2013).

Biber, D., S. Conrad and G. Leech (2002), *The Longman Student Grammar of Spoken and Written English*, London: Longman.

Biddulph, J. (1986), 'A short grammar of Black Country', *Xenododo*, 9: 22–32.

Bounds, J. (2007), 'I make love to a BBC Micro', *Birmingham: It's Not Shit*, <http://www.birminghamitsnotshit.co.uk>

Briggs, K. M. (1991), *A Dictionary of British Folk-Tales in the English Language: Incorporating the F. J. Norton Collection*, London: Routledge, vol. 2, part 1.

Britton, D. (1992), 'Secondary contraction and deletion of negative enclitics in English dialects', *Zeitschrift für Dialektologie und Linguistik*, 59: 38–49.

Brook, G. L. (1972), *English Dialects*, London: Deutsch.

Buchstaller, I. (2004), 'Social stereotypes, personality traits and regional perception displaced: Attitudes towards the 'new' quotatives in the UK', *Journal of Sociolinguistics*, 10: 362–81.

Chambers, J. and P. Trudgill (1998), *Dialectology*, 2nd edn, Cambridge: Cambridge University Press.

Champion, A. G. (1976), 'Evolving patterns of population distribution in England and Wales 1951–71', *Transactions of the Institute of British Geographers*, 1: 401–20.

Chinn, C. (2004), 'Recalling our sayings from days of the past', *Express and Star*, 13 May 2004.

Chinn, C. and S. Thorne (2001), *Proper Brummie: A Dictionary of Birmingham Words and Phrases*, Studley, Warwickshire: Brewin Books.

Chitham, E. (1972), *The Black Country*, London: Longman.

Christian, D. (1991), 'The personal dative in Appalachian speech', in P. Trudgill and J. Chambers (eds), *Dialects of English: Studies in Grammatical Variation*, London: Longman, pp. 10–19.

Clark, U. (2004/2008), 'The English West Midlands: phonology', in E. Schneider, K. Burridge, B. Kortmann, R. Mesthrie and C. Upton (eds), *A Handbook of Varieties of English*, Berlin and New York: Mouton de Gruyter, vol. 1: *Phonology*, pp. 134–62.

Clark, U. (2013), *Language and Identity in Englishes*, London: Routledge.

Cobbett, W. (1893), *Rural Rides*, London: Dent, vol. 2.

Coupland, N. (2007), *Style: Language Variation and Identity*, Cambridge: Cambridge University Press.

Davies, B. and C. Upton (eds) (2013), *Analysing 21st-century British English: Conceptual and Methodological Aspects of the BBC "Voices" project*, London: Routledge.

Eckert, P. (2005), 'Variation, convention and social meaning', paper presented at the Annual Meeting of the Linguistic Society of America, Oakland, CA, 7 Jan 2005, <http://www.stanford.edu/~eckert/EckertLSA2005.pdf> (last accessed 3 March 2006).

Ellis, A. (1889), *On Early English Pronunciation, with Especial Reference to Shakspere and Chaucer*, Part V, London: Trübner and Co.

Feagin, C. (2002), 'Entering the community: Fieldwork', in J. K. Chamber, P. Trudgill and N. Schilling-Estes (eds), *The Handbook of Language Variation and Change*, Oxford: Blackwell.

Fisiak, J. (1968), *A Short Grammar of Middle English*, Warsaw: Państwowe Wydawnictwo Naukowe, vol. 1.

Fletcher, K. (trans.) (1975), *The Old Testament in the Dialect of the Black Country. Part 1, The Books of Genesis to Deuteronomy*, Kingswinford: The Black Country Society.

Freeborn, D. (1998), *From Old English to Standard English*, 2nd edn, London: Palgrave Macmillan.

Freeman, J. (1930), *Black Country Stories and Sketches, Illustrating Life in the Staffordshire Black Country*, Bilston: James Wilkes.

Gale, W. (1966), *The Black Country Iron Industry: A Technical History*, London: The Iron and Steel Institute.

Gibson, P. (1955), 'Studies in the linguistic geography of Staffordshire', unpublished MA dissertation, University of Leeds.

Giddens, A. (1991), *Modernity and Self-Identity: Self and Society in the Late Modern Age*, Cambridge: Polity Press/Blackwell.

Gimson, A. and A. Cruttenden (1994), *Gimson's Pronunciation of English*, 5th edn, London: Arnold.

Hammersley, M and P. Atkinson (2007), *Ethnography: Principles in Practice*, 3rd edn, London: Routledge.

Heath, C. (1971), 'A study of speech patterns in the Urban District of Cannock, Staffordshire', unpublished PhD dissertation, University of Leeds.

Heath, C. (1980), *The Pronunciation of English in Cannock, Staffordshire*, Publications of the Philological Society XXIX, Oxford: Blackwell.

Higgs, L. (2004), *A Description of Grammatical Features and their Variation in the Black Country Dialect*, Basel: Schwabe Verlag. *Sociolinguistics*, 3: 542–56.

Hogg, R. (2000), 'The standardiz/sation of English', paper presented to the Queen's English Society, March 2000.

Holmes, J. and A. Bell (1988), 'Learning by experience: Notes for New Zealand social dialectologists', *Te Reo*, 31: 19–49.Horobin, S. and J. Smith (2011), 'Language', PDF located within W. Scase (ed.), *A Facsimile Edition of the Vernon Manuscript* (DVD), Oxford: Bodleian Digital Texts 3.

Howarth, J. (1988), 'The dialect of Walsall in the West Midlands', unpublished BA dissertation, University of Sheffield.

Hubbard, W. (1960), 'A grammar of the dialect of Albrighton, North East Shropshire', unpublished MA dissertation, University of Leeds.

Hughes, A. and P. Trudgill (1996), *English Accents and Dialects: An Introduction to Social and Regional Varieties of English in the British Isles*, 2nd edn, London: Arnold.

Johnstone, B. (2009), 'Pittsburghese shirts: Commodification and the enregisterment of an urban dialect', *American Speech*, 84: 157–75.

Johnstone, B., J. Andrus and A. E. Danielson (2006), 'Mobility, indexicality, and the enregisterment of "Pittsburghese"', *Journal of English Linguistics*, 32: 77–104.

Johnstone, B. and D. Baumgardt (2004), '"Pittsburghese" online: Vernacular norming in conversation', *American Speech*, 709: 115–235.

Johnstone, B., N. Bhasin and D. Wittkofski (2002), '"Dahntahn" Pittsburgh: Monophthongal /aw/ and representations of localness in southwestern Pennsylvania', *American Speech*, 77: 148–66.

Keogh (2012), 'Birmingham school where 31 languages spoken', *Birmingham Mail online*, 7 June 2012, <http://www.birminghammail.co.uk/news/local-news/birmingham-school-where-31-languages-spoken-186431> (last accessed on 15 March 2013).

Kerswill, P., C. Llamas and C. Upton (1999), 'The first SuRE moves: Early steps towards a large dialect project', *Leeds Studies in English*, 30: 257–69.

Kerswill, P. and A. Williams (1994), 'A new dialect in a new city: Children's and adults' speech in Milton Keynes', final report to the Economic and Social Research Council, May 1994.

Kerswill, P. and A. Williams (2000), 'Creating a new town koine: children and language change in Milton Keynes', *Language in Society*, 29: 65–115.

Khan, A. (2006), 'A sociolinguistic study of Birmingham English', unpublished PhD dissertation, University of Lancaster.

Labov, W. (1966), *The Social Stratification of English in New York City*, Washington: Center for Applied Linguistics.

Labov, W. (1972a), *Sociolinguistic Patterns*, Philadelphia: University of Pennsylvania Press.

Labov, W. (1972b), 'The study of language in its social context', in J. Pride and J. Holmes (eds), *Sociolinguistics*, Harmondsworth: Penguin, pp. 180–201.

Labov, W. (1984), 'Field methods of the Project on Linguistic Change and Variation', in J. Baugh and J. Sherzer (eds.), *Language in Use: Reading in Sociolinguistics*, Englewood Cliffs, NJ: Prentice Hall, pp. 28–66.

Lavandera, B. (1978), 'Where does the sociolinguistic variable stop?', *Language in Society*, 7: 171–82.

Lave, J. and E. Wenger (1991), *Situated Learning: Legitimate Peripheral Participation*, Cambridge: Cambridge University Press.

Lawton, D. (1968), *Social Class, Language and Education*, London: Routledge.

Llamas. C. (2007), '"A place between places": language and identity in a border town', *Language in Society*, 36: 579–604.

Macafee, C. (1994), 'Dialect erosion, with special reference to Urban Scots', in A. Fenton and D. Macdonald (eds), *Studies in Scots and Gaelic: Proceedings of the Third International Conference on the Languages of Scotland*, Edinburgh: Canongate Academic/The Linguistic Survey of Scotland, School of Scottish Studies, University of Edinburgh, pp. 69–80.

Macafee, C. (2003), 'Studying Scots vocabulary', in J. Corbett, D. McClure and J. Stuart-Smith (eds), *The Edinburgh Companion to Scots*, Edinburgh: Edinburgh University Press, pp. 51–71.

Macaulay, R. (2001), 'You're like "why not?" The quotative expressions of Glasgow adolescents', *Journal of Sociolinguistics*, 5: 3–21.

McEntegart, D. and R. Le Page (1978), 'An appraisal of the statistical techniques used in the Sociolinguistic Survey of Multilingual Communities', in P. Trudgill (ed.), *Sociolinguistic Patterns in British English*, London: Arnold, pp. 105–24.

McIntosh, A., M. Samuels and M. Benskin, with M. Laing and K. Williamson (1986), *A Linguistic Atlas of Late Mediæval English*, Aberdeen: Aberdeen University Press, vol. 2: *Item Maps*.

Manley, S. (1971), 'The Black Country dialect in the Cradley Heath area', unpublished MA dissertation, University of Leeds.

Mathisen, A. (1999), 'Sandwell, West Midlands: ambiguous perspectives on gender patterns and models of change', in P. Foulkes and G. Docherty (eds), *Urban Voices: Accent Studies in the British Isles*, London: Arnold, pp. 107–23.

Matthews, P. (2007), *Oxford Concise Dictionary of Linguistics*, 2nd edn, Oxford: Oxford University Press.

Millennium Memory Bank (1999), Recording no. C900/18568 C1, London: The British Library.

Milroy, L. (1987), *Observing and Analysing Natural Language: A Critical Account of Sociolinguistic Method*, Oxford: Blackwell.

Milroy, L. and M. Gordon (2003), *Sociolinguistics: Method and Interpretation*, Oxford: Blackwell, pp. 161–77.

Moore, E. (2006), '"You tell all the stories": using narrative to explore hierarchy within a Community of Practice', *Journal of Sociolinguistics*, 10: 611–40.

Ogden, J. (2005), 'Sharrap, it's our lingo', *Express and Star*, 21 July 2005.

Orton, H. and M. Barry (eds) (1969), *Survey of English Dialects (B): The Basic Material*, Leeds: E. J. Arnold, vol. 2, part 1: *The West Midland Counties*.

Orton, H. and M. Barry (eds) (1970), *Survey of English Dialects (B): The Basic Material*, Leeds: E. J. Arnold, vol. 2, part 2: *The West Midland Counties*.

Orton, H. and M. Barry (eds) (1971), *Survey of English Dialects (B): The Basic Material*, Leeds: E. J. Arnold, vol. 2, part 3: *The West Midland Counties*.

Oxford English Dictionary, 2nd edn (1989), ed J. Simpson and E. Weiner, additions 1993–7 (ed J. Simpson, E. Weiner and M. Proffitt), 3rd edn (in progress) March 2000 (ed. J. Simpson), *OED Online*, Oxford: Oxford University Press, <http://www.oed.com> (last accessed 28 February 2008).

Painter, C. (1963), 'Specimen: Black Country speech', *Le Maître Phonétique*, 119: 30–3.

Palmer, F. R. (1976), *Semantics*, Cambridge: Cambridge University Press.

Parker, D. (1984), *Aynuk and Ayli's Black Country Joke Book*, Tettenhall: Broadside.

Parker, D. (1991), *Black Country Jokes and Humour*, Tettenhall: Broadside.

Parsons, H. (1986), *The Black Country*, London: Robert Hale.

Pollner, K. (1985), 'Old words in a new town', *Scottish Language*, 4: 5–15.

Poole, C. (1880), *An Attempt Towards a Glossary of the Archaic and Provincial Words of the County of Stafford First Brought Together by C. H. Poole AD 1880*, Stratford upon Avon: Saint Gregory's Press.

Quirk, R., S. Greenbaum, G. Leech and J. Svartvik (1985), *A Comprehensive Grammar of the English Language*, London and New York: Longman.

Rampton, B., K. Tusting, J. Maybin, R. Barwell, A. Creese and V. Lytra (2004), 'UK linguistic ethnography: a discussion paper', unpublished.

Raven, J. (1979), *Aynuk's Secund Black Country Waerd Buk*, Tettenhall: Broadside.

Raven, J. and M. Raven (eds) (1965), *Folk out of Focus: Being a Brief Resume of the Little Known Folk Lore of the Black Country and Staffordshire*, Wolverhampton: Wolverhampton Folk Song Club.

Raven, M. and J. Raven (eds) (1966), *Folk-Lore and Songs of the Black Country and West Midlands*, Wolverhampton: Wolverhampton Folk Song Club, vol. 2.

Rees, H. (1946), 'Birmingham and the Black Country', *Economic Geography*, 22: 133–41.

Retrosellers (undated), 'Interview with Janice Nicholls', <http://www.retrosellers.com/features26.htm> (last accessed 12 September 2009).

Rickford, J. (1986), 'The need for new approaches to class analysis in sociolinguistics', *Language and Communication*, 6: 215–21.

Rock, M. (1974), 'A dialect study of Quarry Bank, near Dudley, Worcestershire', *Journal of the Lancashire Dialect Society*, 23: 5–20.

Scase, W. (2011), *The Making of the Vernon Manuscript: The Production and Contexts of Oxford, Bodleian Library, MS Eng. poet. a. 1*, Early Book Society series, Texts and Transitions 6: Studies in the History of Manuscripts and Early Printed Books, Turnhout: Brepols.

Shaw, T. (1930), *A Glossary of Black Country Words and Phrases*, Birmingham: Cornish Bros.

Silverstein, M. (2003), 'Indexical order and the dialectics of social life', *Language and Communication*, 23: 193–229.

Snell, J. (2007), '"Give us my shoe back": the pragmatic functions of singular us', *Leeds Working Papers in Linguistics and Phonetics*, 12: 44–59.

Sweet, H. ([1882] 1995), *The Anglo-Saxon Primer*, 9th edn, rev. throughout by N. Davis, Oxford: Oxford University Press.

Tagliamonte, S. (2006), *Analysing Sociolinguistic Variation*, Cambridge: Cambridge University Press.

Tagliamonte, S. and A. D'Arcy (2004), '*He's like, she's like*: the quotative system in Canadian youth', *Journal of Sociolinguistics*, 8: 493–514.

Tennant, R. (1982), *The Book of Brum, or 'Mekya Selfa Tum'*, Sutton Coldfield: Big in Ink Publishing.

Tennant, R. (1983), *Aware Din Urea: A Second Book of Brum*, Sutton Coldfield: Big in Ink Publishing.

Thorne, S. (2003), 'Birmingham English: a sociolinguistic study', unpublished PhD dissertation, University of Birmingham.

Thorne, S. (2005), 'Accent pride and prejudice: are speakers of stigmatised variants *really* less loyal?', *Journal of Quantitative Linguistics*, 12: 2–3, 151–66.

Todd, L. and S. Ellis (1992) in T. McArthur and F. McArthur (eds), *The Oxford Companion to the English Language*, Oxford: Oxford University Press.

Townsend, P. (1979), *Poverty in the United Kingdom: A Survey of Household Resources and Standards of Living*, Harmondsworth: Penguin.

Toynbee, P. (1998), 'It's cool, it's hip. And soon it will be a testbed of grassroots democracy', *The Guardian*, 20 January 1998.

Trudgill, P. (1990), *The Dialects of England*, illustrated edn, Oxford: Blackwell.

Trudgill, P. (1999), *The Dialects of England*, 2nd edn, Oxford: Blackwell.

Trudgill, P. and J. Chambers (eds) (1991), *Dialects of English: Studies in Grammatical Variation*, London: Longman.

UK Piano Page Piano Discussion Forums (2009), 'Watch this space, folks!', <http://www.uk-piano.org/piano-forums/viewtopic.php?f=18&t=7454> (last accessed 20 September 2009).

Underwood, G. (1988), 'Accent and Identity', in A. Thomas (ed.), *Methods in Dialectology. Proceedings of the Sixth International Conference held at the University College of North Wales, 3–7 August 1987*, Clevedon: Multilingual Matters, pp. 406–27.

Upton, C. and C. Llamas (1999), ' Two large-scale and long-term language variation surveys: a retrospective and a plan', *Cuadernos de filología inglesa*, 8: 291–304.

Wakelin, M. F. (1972), *English Dialects: An Introduction*, London

Walden, I. (email) (2001), 'Re: Black Country - Request for information', email to Esther Asprey.

Wales, K. (1996), *Personal Pronouns in Present-day English*, Cambridge Studies in English Language, Cambridge: Cambridge University Press.

Walker, E. (undated), *The Definitive Black Country Dictionary*, Wednesbury: E. Walker.

Wells, J. (1982a), *Accents of English*, Cambridge: Cambridge University Press, vol. 1: *An Introduction*.

Wells, J. (1982b), *Accents of English*, Cambridge: Cambridge University Press, vol. 2: *The British Isles*.

Williams, A. and Kerswill, P. (1999), 'Dialect levelling and geographical diffusion in British English', in D. Britain and J. Cheshire (eds) (2003), *Social Dialectology: In Honour of Peter Trudgill*, Amsterdam: Benjamins, pp. 223–43.

Wilson, D. (1974), *Staffordshire Dialect Words: A Historical Survey*, Stafford: Staffordshire Moorland Publishing Company.

Wolfram, W. (1991a), 'The Linguistic Variable: Fact and Fantasy', *American Speech*, 66: 22–32.

Wolfram, W. (1991b), 'Towards a description of *a*-prefixing in Appalachian English', in P. Trudgill and J. Chambers (eds), *Dialects of English: Studies in Ggrammatical Variation*, London: Longman, pp. 229–40.

Wolfram, W. and N. Schilling-Estes (1998), *American English*, Oxford: Blackwell.

Woolard, K. (2004), 'Language Ideology: issues and approaches', *Pragmatics*, 2: 235–51.

Workman, L. and H.-J. Smith (2008), 'Yorkshire named top twang as Brummie brogue comes bottom', *The Guardian Online*, <http://www.guardian.co.uk/uk/2008/apr/04/6> (last accessed 7 September 2012).

6 Annotated Texts

Text One: Craig

Craig is a 44 year old white male. He self-declared working/middle class at interview and talked about the difficulty of knowing what social class he belonged to. He attended the University of Hull where he read Modern Languages; he now teaches at secondary level in Birmingham. Apart from his time in Hull and other short spells in Germany and France he has lived all his life in Birmingham; first on the northern side of the city and now more centrally. At the time of recording he was building up a successful second career in stand-up comedy, and this is the focus of the passage, more particularly the reaction of audiences to a Birmingham comedian. Craig's accent is typically younger Birmingham, with glottalling a feature. He eschews any non-standard lexis or grammar for our conversation, though he does use regionalisms in his speech, there are none in this extract. Similarly this relatively formal context elicited no non-standard syntactic or morphological forms.

"No I do at the beginning always mention that I'm from Birmingham and I always make a joke about the fact it never gets a cheer when I say I'm from Birmingham some places genuinely do get a cheer Manchester for example people will often whoop because there's always somebody from Manchester I the crowd if you say you're from Birmingham generally there's a silence occasionally somebody will go ooh or aar or never mind but it's nice it's nice banter in that way and I try to make a joke about it I say it never gets a cheer even when I do gigs in Birmingham they never they don't cheer it's kind of I don't know it's it's this thing that we've got as Brummies that we don't cheer about who we are we're proud of who we are but we don't cheer about it."

/nəʊɑdu:aʔðəbɪgɪnɪnaɪɔ:lwɛzmɛnʃnða?aɪmfrəmbɜːmɪŋɡəmanɑɔ:lwɛɪzmɛɪk
ədʒɔʊkəboʊ?ðəfaʔkðə?ɪʔnɛvagɛtsətʃi:əwɛnjəseɪaɪmfrəmbɜːmɪŋɡəmsʏmplɛ

157

ɪsɪzdʒenju:ɪnlɛɪdu:geʔatʃi:aju:nəʊə:mantʃestəfɹegzamplpi:plwɪlɒfnwu:pkəz
ðɛ:zɔ:lwɛɪzɤmənfrəmmantʃestəɪnðəɪnðəkraʊdbɒʔɪfjəsɛɪamfɹəmbɜ:mɪŋgə
mdʒenɹəlɛɪðɛ:zasaɪlənsəkɛɪʒənəlɪsɤmbədiwɪlgoʊwu:ɔ:ɑ:ɔ:nɛvəmɒɪndbɤɹɪs
naɪsɪtsnaɪsbantaɪnðaʔwɛɪanaɪtɹaɪəmɛɪkədʒoʊkəbaʊɹɪtasɛɪɪʔnɛvagɛtsətʃi:əi:
vnwɛnadu:gɪgzɪnbɜ:mɪŋgəmənɪʔstɹu:ðɛɪnɛvəðɛɪdoʊnʔtʃi:əɪʔskaɪndɒvadʊn
ʊɪʔsðɪsθɪŋgwi:vgɒtazbɹʊmi:zðaʔwi:doʊntʃi:əɹəbaʊʔu:wi:ɑ:wi:pɹaʊdəvhu:
wi:ɑ:bɤʔwi:doʊnʔtʃi:əɹəbaʊtɪt/

Text Two: Paul Jennings

Paul is a 58 year old former police officer. He is a white male who
self-declared working class status at interview. He was born in central
Dudley on the Rosalind Estate, and went to grammar school there,
leaving school at 16 and after a series of manual and semi-manual jobs,
joining the police. He finished his career quite high up the ladder of
promotion and took early retirement to concentrate on performing
stand up comedy. He now lives in Shropshire. The excerpt centres on
his early days in comedy and winning a talent contest, the prize for
which was three support slots with Frank Skinner, the Halesowen born
comedian.

"I turned up this was on I mean this was like years I turned up the
one day at the bear there was this big bloke sitting up the back in a small
bar up the back of the back area in the upstairs room come to have a go
and I went and I did stuff about growing up in the Black Country. Total
stuff off the top of my head stuff that I knew and I stormed it and he he
he said you know this this is his words not mine you're the best open mic
spot I've seen and because of that he gave me er a couple of gigs with
erm your man Frank Skinner so next thing I know and I'm looking back
thinking what a bloody opportunity."

/aɪtɜ:ndʊpðɪswəzɒnami:nðɪswəzlaɪkjiəzaɪɜ:ndʊpðəwɒndeɪaʔðəbɛ:ðɛ:wəzðɪ
sbɪgbloʊkṣɪtɪnʊpðəbækɪnasmɔ:lbɑ:ʊpɪnðəbækəvðəbækɛ:ɹiəɪnðiʊpstɛ:zɹɹu:m
kʊmtu:avagəʊanɑ0wɛntənad0dstʊfəbaʊtgɹɒʊɪnʊpɪnðəblaʔkʊntɹɪtɒʊtlɪtɒpəv
miɛdstʊfðaɹɑnu:anɑ:stɔ:mdɪtandi:i:i:sɛdjənoðɪsðɪsɪzɪzw3:dznɒʔmaɪnjɔ:dəbɛ
stoʊpnmaɪkspɒtɑ:vsi:nanbɪkəzəvðati:geivmi:ə:akʊpləgɪgzwɪðə:mjəmanfɹaŋ
kskinəsoʊneksθɪŋgɑ:noʊanɑ:mlʊkɪnbækθɪnkɪnwɒrablʊdi:ɒpətʃu:nəti:/

Text Three: Carl

Carl is a University professor of History at the University of Birmingham,
as well as a published author of countless volumes of local history and
a presenter on BBC Radio WM [West Midlands]. He is 56 years old,

white, and declared working class status at interview. He grew up in Moseley and has lived all his life in Birmingham; following an earlier career as a bookmaker he changed tack to become an academic. Our conversation here centres on regional accent differences within the City of Birmingham. Carl uses Standard English throughout most of the interview, though there is a possible instance of positive 'were' in the phrase 'the south side were a working class accent.' His pronunciation displays frequently backed onsets to the PRICE diphthong, some h-dropping, and velar nasal plus, though note again the bare nasal in present participles.

"Yes it has changed when I was growing up there was a slight difference between the north side my mom's family are from Aston and I think the Summer Lane Hockley Aston accent was flatter and a bit, ah, er a bit, not stronger, but it was certainly flatter, and the south side working class accent, my Dad's from Sparkbrook, that, Balsall Heath was as broad in terms of pronunciation but didn't have quite the same edge as the northern sound, that's died out... because of all the redevelopments and the merging of people from all over the city. My uncles on the north side and the south side from Sparkbrook and Aston never said *man*, they always said *mon*...and when I've been on the radio and said *old mon* people ring up and complain that I'm putting it on....erm we still say *mom* M-O-M I get very annoyed when people put make it M-U-M it's not M-U-M we're *mom*...er my my uncles both on the north side and the south side never said *floor*, it was *flowa*."

/jɛsɪtaztʃeɪndʒdwɛnɑɪwɒzɜːɡɹoʊɪnʊpðɛːwʊzaslɒɪʔtdɪfɹənsbɪtwiːnðənɔːθsɑɪ dmɑmɒmzfamliəfɹəmastnɑnɑːθɪŋkðəsʊmələɪnhoklɪːastnaksənʔwɒzflataən əbɪʔəbɪʔɜːnɒtstrɒŋgabʊɹɪtwɒzsɜːʔənliflataandðəsɛʊθsɒɪdwɜːkɪŋklasaksənt mɑdadzfrʊmspɑːkbɹʊkðaʔbɔːsəlhiːθwəzɒzbɹɔːdɪntɜːmzəvpɹənʊnsɪɛɪʃnbʊʔ dɪdnhavkwaɪtðəsɛɪmɛdʒazðənɔːðnsɛʊndɔːðaʔsdɑɪdɑʊtbɪkɔːsəvɔːlðəriːdɪvɛl əpmɛntsanddəmɜːdʒɪnəvpiːplfrəmɔːloʊvaðəsɪtɛɪmɒɪʊnklzɒnðənɔːθsɒɪdanð əsɛʊθsɑɪdfrʊmspɑːkbɹʊkənastnnɛvasɛdmandɛɪɔːlwɛzsɛdmɒnandwɛnɒɪvbi nɒnðəɹɛɪdjoʊənsɛdoldmɒnpiːplrɪŋgʊpənkəmplɛɪndɑːmpʊɹɪnɪtɒnɔːmwiːs tɪlsɛɪmɒmɛmɒʊɛmɑːgɛʔvɛɹɪənɒɪdwɛnpiːplpʊʔɔːmɛɪkiʔɛmjuːɛmisnɒʔmʏm wiəmɒmɔːmɑɪʊnklzbɛʊðɒnðənɔːθsɒɪdanðəsɛʊθsɑɪnɛvəsɛdflɔːɹɪtwəzflɛʊə/

Text Four: Fizzog Theatre Group – Deb, Sue and Jackie

These three women make up Fizzog Theatre Group, a Dudley based all-women's theatre collective. This discussion, recorded during their lunchbreak at the Black Country Museum while they were employed there doing street theatre there in period costume, centres on the formation of their group after they met at Dudley College doing a performance and drama course.

Deb is 40, was born in Wordsley near Stourbridge and now lives in Stourbridge. She is white and declared working class origin at interview. Sue is also 40 and from Wordsley, where she still lives. She too is white and declared working class origin when asked.

Jackie is 51 and from Bilston, a more northerly and easterly location in the Black Country. The two other women notice differences in Jackie's informal speech to their own, and in other situations have discussed these with us. Jackie is white and declares working class affiliation at interview.

Sue and Deb's speech is typical of the south of the Black Country, though this semi-formal interview does not elicit grammatical variation or any morphological variation. They both use the glottal stop, h-drop variably and employ velar nasal plus. Jackie's speech contains higher levels of /h/ dropping, though this is not regionally linked, and a tendency to diphthongise in the PRICE set where the other two speakers tend toward the more recessive monophthongisation.

Deb

"…and had a bit of a natter and though who would we like to work with, we thought Jack and Jack came along, and we were working obviously with Louise at the time and erm erm it's just snowballed from there really. We started doing theatre in health and education that was our main thing wasn't it, for years and erm we've sort of changed direction over the last twelve months."

/anadabiɾəvənataənθɔːtuːwʊdwilaɪktəwɜːkwɪðwiθɔːʔdʒaʔkanəːdʒaːkɛɪməlʊ
ŋganwɪwəwɜːkɪnɒbvʲəsɫiːwɪðluːizaʔðətaimanɜːmɜːmɪsdʒʊssnɒʊbɔːldfɹʊmð
eːɹiːɫiwɪstɑːtɪdduinθiːətəɪnelθənɛdʒjəkeiʃnðaʔwəzaːmeinθɪŋgwaːntitfəjiːzən
jiːzanɜːmwɪvsɔːtəʧeindʒdairekʃnɒʊvəðəlastwɛlvmʊnθs/

Sue

"Erm but then other plays that we've done have been specific to the Black Country, like we did a World War Two play which again we've done for a number of years and erm that's how our old lady characters started, because it started off as we were three old ladies being interviewed by a teenager and then we told our stories of our life during the war, and then it kind of went into a scene of us as children those characters as children. Again we've taken that all around Birmingham the Midlands and stuff like that."

/ɜːmbʊtʔðɛnʊðəpleizðəʔwɪvdʊnəvbɪnspəsɪfɪktəðəblakʊntɹilaɪkwɪdɪdəwɜːl dwɔːtuːpleiwɪʧʃəgɛnwɪvdʊnfɹənʊmbəɹəvjiːzandəːmðatsaʊɔʊɹ̩ʊʊldlɛidikarə ktəzstaːtɪdbɪkəzɪtstaːtɪdɒfɒfazwɪwəθɹiːʊ̩ʊ̩dlɛidɪzbiːmɪntəvjuːdbaɹətiːnɛɪʤ əandðɛnwɪtoʊldaːstɔːɹiːzɒvlaifʤuːɹɪnðəwɔːanðɛnɪtkaɪndəwɛntɪntuwasiːnɒ vʊzazʧʃ̩ildɹənðoʊzkarɪktəzəzɪldɹ̩nəgɛnwɪvtɛɪknðatɔːɫəɹaunbɜːmɪŋgəmðəmɪd lənzənstʊflaikðat/

Jackie : And er 'black by day' was obviously a term used black by day red by night was the whole birth of the Industrial Revolution with all the soot and the dirt during the day from the furnaces everywhere was just covered in grime so it was black by day and then at night with all the furnaces going I can't remember where I saw it down at Ironbridge Museum on a poster.

/anɜːblakbaideiwəzɒbvjəsliatɜːmjuːzdblakbaideiɹɛdbainaitwəzðəhoʊłbɜːθə vðɪɪndʊʃtɹɪəɫɹɛvəluːʃnwɪðɔːłðəsʊtanðədɜːtʤuːɹɪŋgðədɛɪfɹʊmðəfɜːnɪsɪzɛvɹɪ wɛːwəzʤʊstkʊvədɪŋgɹaɪmsoʊɪtwəzblakbaɪdeɪanðɛnətnaɪtwɪðɔːłðəfɜːnɪsɪz goʊɪnaːkaːnɹ̩ɪmɛmbəwɛːasɔːɪtdaʊnətaɪənbəɹɪʤmuːziːmɒnəpoʊsta/

Deb: I think it's being ebbed away because like years ago you were brought up and you lived in the same not far from you know your parents or whatever people now move away early on and then it just gets diluted and people moved into a new area so to have like pure you know that accent going generation genera- I don't I don't think that happens has happened is happening any more.

/aθɪŋkɪtsbiːmebdəwɛɪbɪkəzlaɪkjɹəzəgoʊjuwəbɹɔːtʊpanjuːlɪvdɪnðəsɛɪmnɒtʃ aːfɹəmjənoʊjɔːpɛːɹəntsɔːwɒɹɛvənaʊpiːpɫmuːvəwɛɪɜːliɒnanðɛnɪtʤʊsgɛtsda ɪluːtɪdandpiːpɫmuːvdɪntuːənuːɛɹɪəsoʊtuːavlaɪkpjuːjənoʊðataksəntgoʊɪndʒɛ nəɹɛɪʃndʒɛnəɹɛɪaɪdoʊntadoʊnθɪŋkðatapnzhazhapndizhapninɛnimɔː/

Index

Note: page numbers in *italics* denote figures or tables